"Daniel Hill sought me out as a mentor over two decades ago, and it has been a joy to watch the progress of him and his church. Now, in *White Awake*, he shares lessons learned on his journey of following Jesus into the ministry of reconciliation. As Christians in this day and age, we all need to think critically and closely examine the teachings of Scripture. In this book, you will find fresh thinking around the critical topic of race, and I would encourage every Christian to read it."

John M. Perkins, author, cofounder of the Christian Community Development Association

"*White Awake* is a profoundly pastoral book with serious implications for the ecclesial, social, and political life of our nation. At a time when conversations about race seem increasingly cross-pressured by various interests and motivations, readers can trust Daniel Hill to tell them the truth about racism and white supremacy. . . . I'm grateful to Daniel for writing *White Awake*."

Michael Wear, author of *Reclaiming Hope*

"Daniel Hill has been my friend for almost two decades, and with each passing year, I learn more from him and admire him more. His passion, intelligence, and depth are gifts to the community he pastors and to the city of Chicago, and this book is a wise and helpful guide for all of us who want to learn more about both the theology and practice of reconciliation in America today."

Shauna Niequist, author of *Present Over Perfect*

"Daniel Hill's personal and deep dive into whiteness, reconciliation, and the dividing lines in our social matrix of race is needed like never before. At a time of ongoing racial weariness and colorblind responses, I'm so grateful for this resource. Allow the transparency and courage of this book to lead you into the needed work of unity, liberation, and justice."

Efrem Smith, author of *Killing Us Softly* and *The Post-Black and Post-White Church*

"*White Awake* is at once personal, practical, and provocative. Well conceived, researched, and written, this timely book provides a detailed consideration of cultural identity and its formation from which everyone can benefit—particularly those of us who are white and willing to engage the topic not only for our own benefit but, more significantly, for the sake of the gospel, as ambassadors of Christ and ministers of reconciliation in an increasingly diverse society."

Mark DeYmaz, founding pastor of Mosaic Church, author of *Building a Healthy Multi-Ethnic Church*

"*White Awake* is both a poignant academic analysis of race and the dominant culture in America and a practical and clear path for others to navigate the experience, disorientation, and ultimate awakening that comes with deep reflection on white racial identity. This book has rightfully earned a place on my bookshelf and in my list of recommended books—I'm confident it will earn a similar spot in yours as well."

Ken Wytsma, founder of The Justice Conference, author of *The Myth of Equality* and *Create vs. Copy*

"*White Awake* is a crucial book for our time, as the social and political landscape progresses into torrential territories. This book is challenging, provocative, and significant, and I strongly recommend it."

Grace Ji-Sun Kim, associate professor of theology, Earlham School of Religion, author of several books, including *Embracing the Other* and *Mother Daughter Speak*

"In *White Awake*, Daniel Hill humbly and insightfully shares his personal journey of understanding race and privilege. He provides a practical and challenging look at the blinders and barriers that hinder racial reconciliation and our ability to advocate for equity and justice for all. I am grateful for this resource that helped me better understand where I am in my own journey and how I can more effectively challenge myself and my church to be active participants in furthering the Jesus mission of reconciliation and restoration."

Dave Ferguson, lead pastor, Community Christian Church, lead visionary, NewThing

"For about two decades, Daniel Hill has been wrestling with what it means to be a white man in America and a white pastor in the city of Chicago. He is fearlessly curious and inquisitive. When things get uncomfortable, he leans in. This book is Daniel's invitation to lean into the current moment and join the movement for racial justice—lest we discover a generation from now that we slept through a revolution."

Shane Claiborne, author and activist

"Many evangelicals of color have grown weary of ringing the bell and issuing the clarion call for racial justice. While we do not look for white evangelicals to legitimize or affirm our perspective, it's nice on occasion to know that there are 'woke' white evangelicals out there. It's nice to know that these efforts have not been in vain. Daniel Hill has been my friend and ally for many years. In this book, you will have the chance to hear his story and heart—and learn from a learner."

Soong-Chan Rah, North Park Theological Seminary, author of *The Next Evangelicalism* and *Prophetic Lament*

"Have you ever been awakened to a new reality? In *White Awake*, my friend Daniel Hill bravely reimagines St. Paul's call to awake from slumber. Hill's confession is a courageous call for Christians to respond faithfully to discipleship's demands, beyond guilt and shame, toward racial justice, reconciliation, and action. His journey will doubtlessly awaken others!"

Gabriel Salguero, president, National Latino Evangelical Coalition

"We are waking up to the reality that the construct of race that elevates whiteness as superior is destroying us all, regardless of ethnicity. *White Awake* helps us slay this giant and regain the hope that is found in Christ to see all people as magnificently created in the image of God. Thank you, Daniel, for your courage and for writing this book."

Noel Castellanos, president of the Christian Community Development Association, author of *Where the Cross Meets the Street*

White Awake

An honest look at what it means to be white

DANIEL HILL

Foreword by **Brenda Salter McNeil**

IVP Books

An imprint of InterVarsity Press
Downers Grove, Illinois

InterVarsity Press
P.O. Box 1400, Downers Grove, IL 60515-1426
ivpress.com
email@ivpress.com

InterVarsity Press® is the book-publishing division of InterVarsity Christian Fellowship/USA®, a movement of students and faculty active on campus at hundreds of universities, colleges, and schools of nursing in the United States of America, and a member movement of the International Fellowship of Evangelical Students. For information about local and regional activities, visit intervarsity.org.

All Scripture quotations, unless otherwise indicated, are taken from The Holy Bible, New International Version®, NIV®. Copyright © 1973, 1978, 1984, 2011 by Biblica, Inc.™ Used by permission of Zondervan. All rights reserved worldwide. www.zondervan.com. The "NIV" and "New International Version" are trademarks registered in the United States Patent and Trademark Office by Biblica, Inc.™

While any stories in this book are true, some names and identifying information may have been changed to protect the privacy of individuals.

Published in association with the literary agency of Mark Sweeney & Associates.

Cover design: Cindy Kiple
Interior design: Daniel van Loon
Images: abstract crowd: © Diana Ong/Getty Images. Image used for illustrative purposes only.
     page curl: © Fosin2/iStockphoto

ISBN 978-0-8308-4393-0 (print)
ISBN 978-0-8308-8913-6 (digital)

Printed in the United States of America ♾

InterVarsity Press is committed to ecological stewardship and to the conservation of natural resources in all our operations. This book was printed using sustainably sourced paper.

Library of Congress Cataloging-in-Publication Data
Names: Hill, Daniel, 1973- author.
Title: White awake : an honest look at what it means to be white / Daniel
   Hill ; foreword by Brenda Salter McNeil.
Description: Downers Grove : InterVarsity Press, 2017. | Includes
   bibliographical references.
Identifiers: LCCN 2017038101 (print) | LCCN 2017033974 (ebook) | ISBN
   9780830889136 (eBook) | ISBN 9780830843930 (pbk. : alk. paper)
Subjects: LCSH: Race--Religious aspects--Christianity. | Whites--Race
   identity. | Race awareness.
Classification: LCC BT734 (print) | LCC BT734 .H55 2017 (ebook) | DDC
   277.3/08308909--dc23
LC record available at https://lccn.loc.gov/2017038101

P   22   21   20   19   18   17   16   15   14   13   12   11   10   9   8   7   6   5   4

Y   35   34   33   32   31   30   29   28   27   26   25   24   23   22   21   20   19   18

Contents

Foreword

Brenda Salter McNeil

As Christians, we must embark upon an awakening journey—a path that will lead us into direct confrontation with the narrative of racial difference. We must open our eyes to the uncomfortable racial hierarchy that has been the basis for the structure of our entire society. We must wake up to the ways that the narrative of racial difference played a major role in identity formation in the early days of our country, and to the ways it continues to play a dominant role in our sense of identity here and now.

One of the primary issues we must face, especially in this sociopolitical climate, is the need for white people to do the hard work of wrestling with what it really means to be white.

This points to one of the core messages of *White Awake*: the poisonous impact of the narrative of racial difference does not land solely on people of color. The narrative of racial difference has also profoundly affected white people. But unlike people of color, most white people remain completely unaware of the ways this narrative has affected their sense of identity. I often see this as a college professor working with young white students who are eager to engage in the work of reconciliation but who seldom realize the degree to which they are also in bondage to the system of race. I am convinced that until they go through a Holy Spirit–led process of awakening, they will remain in a state of blindness.

I believe that Daniel Hill is God's person to lead them into this life-changing process. I have known and walked with Daniel, the founding pastor of River City Community Church in the Humboldt Park neighborhood of Chicago, for over ten years. I've observed him in many situations and conversations about reconciliation and justice, and I can attest that he is attuned to his own identity and privilege as a white man. Daniel is not seeking attention for doing and saying what he believes to be right and just. In fact, he was reluctant to write this book at all because he didn't want to be another white person taking up the space that he would have preferred to cede to a person of color. I have seen his convictions and understanding of whiteness stir up both deep emotions and negative visceral reactions in those who have heard him share his heart. He knows that the risk of being misunderstood is great, but despite his initial doubts, he came to recognize that he has been uniquely called to write this timely and sorely needed book.

White Awake is a call to tell the truth. It is a call to follow Jesus. It is a call to find our deepest sense of identity in Christ, but also to realize that those who are white can't get there without breaking free of the distorted sense of identity they have internalized from the narrative of racial difference.

This book will lead people on a transformational journey. As you encounter Daniel's story of wrestling with his own ethnic identity, I hope that his honest reflections create a safe environment for others to embark on a similar path. For those who take the journey, this book has the potential to change hearts and minds and help Christians reclaim a message of reconciliation that repairs our interracial relationships and the structures that mediate those relationships. Let the awakening to racial and social healing begin!

The Day I Discovered My World Was White

It was a cold December weekend in Chicago, and I was excited. One of my best friends was getting married, and to top it off, he had asked me to officiate the wedding. I was honored by the invitation, though a bit intimidated. What if I botched it and ended up being the guy the editor tried to remove from all the film footage? I was a brand-new pastor and had been in vocational ministry for less than a year, and this was my first wedding.

My friend, the groom, was of South Asian/Indian descent, and he was very proud of his cultural heritage. He had promised that the reception in particular would take guests on a deep dive into Indian culture and that we should prepare ourselves for a culturally unique experience. The reception lived up to the hype, and I had a night to remember. My personal highlight was the *dandiya* dance, a group of people moving in two circles counterclockwise, holding two colorful sticks. I'm typically hesitant to get out on the dance floor, but the beauty of the dandiya was compelling.

When the dance ended, I was still feeling festive from the amazing experience. So I found my friend and shared with him how much I had enjoyed every bit of that wonderful night. Then I innocently added a comment: "I'm jealous of you. You have such an amazing culture! It must be such a privilege to be able to reflect that beautiful culture during your wedding weekend. I wish I had a culture too."

I had no idea how much was packed into that little statement, but it sure wasn't lost on him. He suddenly got serious, placed his hand on my shoulder, and looked me straight in the eye. "Daniel, you may be white, but don't let that lull you into thinking you have no culture. White culture is very real. In fact, when white culture comes in contact with other cultures, it almost always wins. So it would be a really good idea for you to learn about your culture."

I found myself revisiting this conversation often. My friend was known for avoiding serious topics, so I had been surprised by the spontaneous intensity he had displayed. Most unsettling about it was his commentary on my "white" culture. First of all, I felt he was lumping me in with every other white person he'd ever known. I thought, *He can't seriously think there's just one white culture, can he?* In an attempt to piece together the confusing message he'd sent my way, I reflected on the Irish heritage on my father's side and the pride many of my relatives took in it. Then I thought about the German and French heritage on my mom's side. I knew less about those cultures, but still, they were three very different backgrounds. Was he suggesting that those three distinct cultures could be mashed into a single category: white? That seemed like a major stretch.

Then there was the even more unsettling suggestion that my culture wins whenever it comes in contact with another. Not only was he lumping all white cultures into a single group, he was also proposing that this single conglomeration consistently dominates other cultures. How would this not come off as insulting to a white person?

What seemed utterly obvious to him was utterly confusing to me. But I wanted to give him the benefit of the doubt, and I searched for where I could find agreement with him. I could readily acknowledge that some white individuals exhibit dominant or even racist behaviors. Certainly that was common ground.

But even then I found myself thinking, *Just because certain white individuals demonstrate prejudice or racism by their behaviors doesn't implicate an entire race.* I guessed that he would respond poorly to the suggestion that certain individuals of Indian heritage represent their entire race. Yet he seemed comfortable with the idea of poorly behaved white individuals representing all white people.

This monologue continued to live inside my head longer than expected, and I anxiously awaited its end. Instead it grew in intensity. I wasn't sure why, but it was becoming clear that God had provoked something in me through this brief encounter. My friend had opened a monumental door and had left me to decide whether or not to step through it. He had opened me up to a whole new world, but I was unable to navigate it on my own.

The Quest

Compelled by these unanswered questions, I began reading books and articles, listening to TED talks, and talking with anyone who appeared knowledgeable about this topic. While a number of interesting ideas were planted in the soil of my mind during that time, a conversation with an eventual mentor led to my initial epiphany. I'd had no previous relationship with this mentor, and after a steady series of my requests, he kindly agreed to meet with me. I wasted no time; I immediately peppered him with questions. I told him about the conversation with my friend at the wedding and shared my confusion about the claim that I was part of a larger white culture that dominates every other culture it comes in contact with.

He patiently sat there, listening as I verbally sorted out my thoughts and feelings. When I finally finished, I pulled out my notebook, eager for answers. I was curious to hear his insights into these dilemmas and was ready to engage with his ideas.

But he didn't respond to my questions at an abstract, intellectual level. Instead he issued a personal challenge in the form of a reflection exercise. To help me begin my exploration, he invited me to catalog carefully the primary voices that informed me as a person and shaped my thoughts and values. To simplify, he organized the exercise around four groups of voices: my closest friends, the mentors I looked to for guidance, the preachers/teachers/theologians I relied on for spiritual guidance, and the authors of the books I was reading.

The instructions were simple:

♦ Comprehensively list them.

♦ Take note of the cultural backgrounds they represented.

Just How White My World Was

I started with my friendship circle, just as he'd asked. Though I had some acquaintances in my broader network from diverse cultural backgrounds, I couldn't include them as *close* friends. So I made my list, and everyone on it was white.

Next up were my mentors, those I looked up to for advice during challenging times. It didn't take long to develop this list, as I quickly surmised that I consistently went to six different people when I needed guidance. When I listed them and noted what culture they represented, I realized they too were all white.

The third category took the longest. I had become a serious student of the Bible by this point, so I listened to many preachers, teachers, and theologians. I wanted to ensure that my accounting was comprehensive, so I meticulously filed my way through the full archive of cassette tapes and CDs I'd accumulated. I had been encouraged to explore a diverse range of theological perspectives, so I had been influenced by everything from Pentecostals to Presbyterians. But I was stunned to discover that, with the exception of two preachers, the entire roster was white.

The last category I had been instructed to assess was authors, and by that point I was sure of the conclusion. I followed through on the exercise just to be sure, but the results in all four categories were the same: the voices shaping me were overwhelmingly white.

There's no crisp way to summarize all I learned during that self-assessment. I was awakening to a reality that had always been there, hidden in plain sight, but I finally had the eyes to see it:

- My closest friends were white.

- My most trusted mentors were white.

- The teachers and theologians shaping me were white.

- The authors planting new ideas in my mind were white.

- The church I worked at was white.

Just like all moments of genuine awakening, the discovery was both liberating and terrifying: liberating in the way truth always is, lifting you out of the fog and into the light, and terrifying because this revelation of truth demanded changes.

I no longer had the luxury of living in ignorance, feeling good about myself while being blissfully unaware of the cultural influences in my life. I had naively thought that my personal transformation had happened the moment I chose to follow Christ. But I saw clearly in that shifting season of my life that the work was just beginning.

Flying Blind

I was working at Willow Creek Community Church, a megachurch in the Chicago area, when I experienced my first racial awakening described in the previous chapter. At the time, Willow Creek's seeker-sensitive approach was redefining the ministry philosophy of numerous congregations. So there was a tremendous demand for training, equipping, and practical resources. This led to the founding of a companion organization called the Willow Creek Association, and these two entities partnered to run a steady stream of conferences all year long.

The conferences were a sight to behold. I watched in amazement as thousands of church leaders streamed in from across the country, ready and eager to learn. They toured the facility, interrogated the staff, and took tedious notes during the plenary sessions. It was obvious that Willow Creek was making a major impact on the North American church.

The impact of these conferences wasn't limited to church leaders who traveled thousands of miles to attend. Willow Creek was also a major source of inspiration and equipping for me, and I credit it with being the place where most of my leadership skills were honed and developed. A huge job perk of working at Willow Creek was being able to attend these conferences, and I rarely missed one.

But as much as the environment of Willow Creek had shaped me and as much as these conferences had built my leadership skills, I was feeling lost. I had experienced the beginnings of a racial awakening, but I was in need of someone to guide me into the next step of the journey. The question "What am I supposed to do?" burned within me, and I was desperate to find answers.

At the time, I was working on the staff of Axis, a young-adult ministry that was dedicated to reaching twenty-somethings. Other members of the staff were wrestling with issues of race and cultural identity as well, so we committed to reading some books and discussing them together. One of the authors who challenged our thinking was Dr. Michael Emerson, at the time a professor at Rice University as well as a leading scholar on race and religion. His book *Divided by Faith* played a significant role in the racial awakening of Pastor Bill Hybels, who encouraged the entire congregation to read it.

One of the themes that jumped out at me was the *hypersegregation* of the white American church, a term Emerson and his colleagues coined when researching racial segregation in cities. They measured each city based on a range from zero (complete racial *integration*) to one (complete racial *segregation*). If a city measured 0.90 or higher, 90 percent of one group would have to switch neighborhoods to achieve integration; in that case, the city was hypersegregated. A score that high indicated a city's racial makeup. As Emerson said, "Values this high could usually only be achieved through laws, discriminatory lending and real estate procedures, threats, and other racially unequal practices."[1] It was sad but not surprising to see that a number of cities in America approached the value of 0.90.

I was vaguely familiar with the racial history of our country, so it seemed plausible that certain cities still reflected the effects of unjust laws, procedures, and practices. What I didn't expect, though, was that this level of racial segregation reached beyond just cities; it was present in the American church as well. Emerson and team applied the same research criteria when studying congregations and discovered that conservative Protestantism *exceeded* these values of 0.90. This seemed statistically impossible, which led Emerson to suggest, "Even if someone were in control of all conservative Protestantism and had the power and will to consciously assign whites and nonwhites to separate congregations across the nation, obtaining a value of over 0.90 would be a difficult feat. . . . Such segregation values are astonishing."[2]

Revelations like this fueled my desire to find a way to break out of the white-centric world I had been in my whole life and to pursue a more multicultural reality. I began to evangelize enthusiastically about this vision within Willow Creek, though many had been passionate about it long before. In the naiveté of youth, I quickly became the annoying, self-righteous white guy. I felt I had finally seen the light, and I was determined to make everyone around me see it.

The tension I felt due to my growing racial awareness continued to intensify, and it was clear to me that something was going to have to change. Fortunately, around that time an intriguing opportunity presented itself, which created the seemingly perfect next step. The Axis ministry had been growing at breakneck speed; in only five years, it had transformed from a small group to a ministry attracting more than 1,200 to its services weekly. One of the exciting outcomes was a buzz about Axis among young adults. It had become the place to be for twenty-somethings, and we were attracting scores of new visitors each week.

This buzz was reaching all the way into the city of Chicago. Willow Creek's main campus is more than thirty miles from the city limits, and a one-way trip can take as long as ninety minutes with traffic. Nobody on our staff had expected young adults to make that far of a commute, but a small number of urban dwellers were proving us wrong. This provided my supervisor at Willow Creek with a chance to accomplish two goals at the same time: to create a landing spot in the city that kept urban newcomers feeling connected to Axis and to find a way to focus my righteous indignation around diversity. So my job description was rearranged to free up time to launch a new community as an extension of Axis in the city.

A Dream and a Disappointment

I quickly went into action, identifying recruits from the group of city dwellers that were commuting to Axis. I sat down with them one-on-one and pitched the vision for this new community. And I was always sure to emphasize the multicultural piece, as this felt nonnegotiable. I told them all about my own racial epiphany as a white person and encouraged them to seek the same if it hadn't already happened.

This testimony resonated with a number of people, and a launch team formed shortly after. We named the new ministry Metro 212 (Bill Hybels often used the metaphor of 212 degrees to describe spiritual transformation, as that is the temperature at which liquid water turns to steam). Our vision statement centered on loving God, loving our urban neighbors, and being intentional around the pursuit of cultural diversity.

The launch group spent twelve weeks praying, planning, and preparing, and we could hardly wait. We told all our friends about it and invited every Chicagoan we knew to come to the launch. The energy was palpable, and we looked forward to a move of God.

The grand opening was festive and alive, and we had an amazing turnout: our launch team was made up of ten invested individuals, and through their invitations another seventy-five came. Yet as exciting as the grand opening was, I could hardly conceal my disappointment. My dream for Metro 212 was wrapped up in my dream for cultural diversity, and it was clearly not coming to fruition. This was an all-white group.

I felt guilty for feeling disappointed and was conflicted about how to handle it. I could see the significance of so many new people coming, and I didn't want to diminish the work of God that was happening.

Just as importantly, I wanted to be cautious not to shame people for being white. I loved the core team, and I was sure I would love the newcomers. I knew they mattered deeply to God, and I trusted they were being sincere when they said they shared the vision with me. Despite all of this, I couldn't shake the disappointment.

I also couldn't help wondering what I had done wrong in the creation of Metro 212. I had been sincerely asking the question, "What am I supposed to do?" and I had continued to hear how important it was for white people to pursue racial reconciliation and cultural diversity. I had heeded the call, and I had given the new ministry everything I had. Yet, despite my best efforts, I was experiencing little to no success.

Facing Failure

This was the first moment in the journey when I began to suspect that I was flying blind. To that point I had been sustained by passion for the cause, conviction about its importance, and confidence that God would lead us to a new multicultural reality. I was starting to feel wobbly, uncertain, and unresolved. I felt like I was approaching a crossroads, but I didn't know what the alternative directions were.

Looking back, I wish I'd paid closer attention to the signs during that time. I wish I'd reflected on my feelings, questioned my motivations, and examined the early fruit. But by that point I was very invested in the dream, and things were already moving fast with Metro 212, so I didn't have a lot of time to process. Therefore, I doubled down and pushed even harder toward the vision of cultural diversity.

My next move was to establish a mandate that every gathering have people on stage that represented cultural diversity. While this seemed like an obvious thing to do if we were going to pursue our vision, it immediately created complications. I didn't have an internal pool of voices to draw from, so I had no choice but to go outside. This alienated a lot of the core folks because they felt they were being penalized for being white. It was also an expensive proposition, as we didn't have a budget for hiring outside help. Making this happen required a major sacrifice of my personal funds.

My follow-up move was to lean heavily into what I'd heard Hybels refer to as "directional preaching." He believed that the primary way congregants embrace new ideas is through an encounter with Scripture. So I began preaching/teaching on racial reconciliation on an almost weekly basis at Metro 212, so much so that some of the core folks began to wonder about me. There was a concern that I had reversed the priorities of the gospel with my desire for multiculturalism, and this concern was conveyed back to Willow Creek leadership. But I kept preaching away.

Despite all my best efforts, there was almost no movement on the multicultural front. We continued to grow numerically, passing the two hundred mark in attendance, but none of that mattered to me anymore—even if it did get the attention of others. I was trying to create something different—something new. I believed to the core of my being that I needed to participate in a multicultural faith community, and I thought we were capable of doing it. But at the end of the day, I was simply reproducing what I had learned at Willow Creek.

I became desperate for solutions, yet I was unable to figure out why we couldn't diversify Metro 212. We were in the heart of the city. We had a vision statement saturated with the language of cultural diversity. We taught about it, prayed about it, and dreamed about it. We were investing financially. I knew something was missing, but I had no idea where to begin an internal audit of my failure to create a multicultural community. I needed help but didn't know where to turn.

Searching for a Lifeline

I was starting to fall into a downward spiral when a lifeline was thrown my way—or so it seemed. A leader in the African American community had been watching the growth of Metro 212, and he knew how intensely I was pursuing cultural diversity. He reached out and asked if I would like him to set up a meeting with some pastors in the city who were involved in the ministry of racial reconciliation. It sounded like an exact answer to my prayers, so I enthusiastically accepted his offer.

I was more eager than ever to figure out what I was supposed to do, and I hoped that the meeting would become the defining moment of my multicultural ministry call. I knew it was a privilege to sit down with seasoned pastors who knew the city well, and I had a feeling it was going to be a turning point.

When the meeting finally came, I found myself bubbling with anticipation. These four pastors were not only influential but also effectively reaching populations that I was missing at Metro 212. They gave me the floor to open the meeting, and I poured out my heart about the vision of the ministry. I then told them about the challenges I was facing and the confusion I was dealing with. Then I begged them to help me crack the code.

When I finished talking, I pulled out my notebook and prepared to furiously record their advice on what I should do next.

The Latino pastor responded first: "I appreciate your enthusiasm, and I want to get behind you. But I'm having difficulty interacting with your ideas because so much of what you say sounds paternalistic. Why do you think rich white people need to come save us poor brown people?"

His comments felt like a punch in the gut, and I had to work to catch my breath. To make things worse, I had no idea what *paternalistic* meant. But I was certain from his tone that it must not be good.

The Asian American pastor responded next: "You keep talking about building a multicultural ministry, yet everything you just said about race was couched in black/white language. What, if anything, do you know about the different Asian histories and cultures? What makes you think you can effectively reach them through your ministry?"

I was still staggering from the previous comment, and I didn't know how to respond to the new one either. I jotted something down in my notebook about needing to study the histories of different Asian American communities, but I knew that the outcomes of this meeting were going to require more of me than something like that.

The white pastor was the third to respond: "I've seen dozens of pastors like you come and go. You think you're going to change the world, and then you bail as soon as it gets tough. I'll be shocked if you are still here in five years." I tried to think of something from his comments to record in my notebook, but all I did was sit there with a dumbfounded expression.

At this point the black pastor tenderly put his hand on my shoulder, and I hoped and prayed he would say something that would provide reprieve from the shock and awe I was experiencing. He and I had met briefly before, as he was one of the few African American professors at the seminary I had attended. He was also a prolific author on racial reconciliation, and I had meticulously studied his books.

He looked me in the eye and said, "Your vision is really noble. I wish more young pastors were thinking like this. But I also think you need to be realistic. With the racial history in Chicago, there is no chance black people are going to attend a church with a white pastor. So why punish yourself like this? I write books on this stuff, but my own children wouldn't attend a church like that."

I'm not sure what I had expected to happen when I met with those four pastors. I suppose I had a fantasy that they would each tell me how amazing my vision was and then give me the magic solution for creating cultural diversity. But even if I'd downsized my expectations, nothing could have prepared me for the disappointment that came from that meeting.

One day, in the middle of wrestling with my emotions, I finally experienced a major breakthrough. I was reading through the book of John devotionally when I came upon the conversation between Jesus and Nicodemus in chapter three. As a pastor's kid, I had heard this story over and over, but I'd never felt any personal resonance with it. For one, I had always read the encounter as the story of a highly religious person who didn't feel religious enough, but that was never my story; I had always resonated with stories like that of the prodigal son, who was always fighting off tendencies toward disobedience. Also, the heart of their conversation centered on the need to be "born again," and I had an aversion to that phrase. It seemed more like a weapon in the culture wars than a genuine mode of spiritual transformation, so I had screened it out of my vocabulary.

But something about the space and time I was in had positioned me to see this encounter from a new vantage point. I realized that when Nicodemus came to Jesus, he was asking the question I had been asking when I met with those four pastors: "What am I supposed to do?"

From Blindness to Sight

According to John's telling, Nicodemus was an honorable and esteemed man. First, we're told that he was a Pharisee, which gives us a window into how serious he was about religious devotion. Pharisees were distinguished by their strict observance of the Old Testament law and were often commended for their simple lifestyle, harmonious dealings with others, and respect for their elders. Second, we're told that he was a member of the Jewish ruling council (John 3:1), which shows us how sociopolitically involved he was; councils existed everywhere Jews lived, but the ruling council in Jerusalem was a supreme court that presided over them all.

So we can see that Nicodemus had a lot of reasons to feel self-confident. Based on just about any human evaluation, he was an established, venerate figure in the community.

Yet something was still missing for Nicodemus, a fact confirmed in his meeting with Jesus. When he looked at Jesus, he witnessed the incarnation of what he longed for. In particular, he observed a level of spiritual depth and connection that went beyond anything he had ever encountered (John 3:2), and he wanted to experience it for himself. So Nicodemus sought Jesus under the cover of night to find out more.

Unlike some of the other Pharisees, who attempted to trap Jesus with manipulative questions, Nicodemus was sincere and effusive when they met. He authentically heaped praises on Jesus and seemed eager to learn from this spiritual master. He left the conversation open for Jesus to respond as he saw fit, though I doubt there was any scenario in which he could have ever predicted what Jesus would say: "Very truly I tell you, no one can see the kingdom of God unless they are born again" (John 3:3).

How discombobulated Nicodemus must have felt when he heard those words! He didn't perceive himself as a newborn looking for direction but as a seasoned practitioner who had long ago solidified the religious foundation of his life. As a Pharisee, he had a structured routine of the rules, regulations, and religious practices. All that was missing was that last bit of advice, that extra *something* that would push him over the edge. Using the language that had been rattling around in my heart and mind, Nicodemus was essentially asking, "What am I supposed to do?" He was looking for concrete direction from the guru named Jesus in the hopes that he could ascend to the next level in his religious development.

But when Jesus finally spoke, it was clear that they were having two different conversations. Jesus wasn't interested in giving Nicodemus a to-do list. Nor was he interested in affirming the religious foundation that Nicodemus believed was already secured and settled. In fact, based on the comprehensive nature of what Jesus said, it's clear that he was unwilling to acknowledge *any* part of Nicodemus's paradigm.

When Jesus told Nicodemus that no one can *see* the kingdom without a spiritual rebirth, he said something pervasive and far-reaching as well as confrontational, potentially insulting, and even inflammatory. Jesus told Nicodemus that while he may be religiously, socially, and politically accomplished, none of those accomplishments could obscure the fact that he was spiritually *blind*. Nicodemus was a big shot in his world, but if he wanted to enter into Jesus' world, he would have to start from the very beginning.]

An analysis like this might not rattle the cage of someone who already knows he or she is blind, but it must have been incredibly disorienting for an established figure like Nicodemus. It not only called into question his path moving forward but also created a comprehensive critique of everything he had accomplished up to that moment. Jesus was saying that Nicodemus's every good deed, every act of service, and every disciplined response to the law had been performed in a state of blindness.

Nicodemus's confusion had suddenly become easy for me to identify with, as I saw so much of my story in his. He had intended to chart a path forward, but Jesus was calling into question everything Nicodemus had done to get to that point.

I began to consider that I might have done the same thing— confidently plunging toward my vision of success with little regard for whether or not I was seeing clearly. So I reluctantly started retracing my steps, starting with the light-bulb moment about my world being all white and continuing through the launch of Metro 212. I tried to be courageous enough to ask some tough questions:

- Why was it that, upon my discovery of racial injustice, I immediately went into action?

- How was it that I had learned to elevate the question "What am I supposed to do?" over other critical questions?

- Why did I feel comfortable taking on the role of self-proclaimed prophet within my ministry at Willow Creek?

- What made me think I was ready to launch a ministry that would be able to become multicultural?

◆ When I started Metro 212, what racial problems was I attempting to address?

◆ How did I think starting Metro 212 was going to address those racial problems?

Dwelling on these questions—and the lack of answers I had to them—made it easy for me to imagine the embarrassment Nicodemus felt. Like him, I had succumbed to overconfidence in the foundation I was operating from. And, like him, I was oblivious to what I didn't even know. I was blind, but I didn't know I was blind.

And that's the most dangerous blindness of all.

Learning to Ask the Right Question

As I learned to see myself in the story of Nicodemus, I felt ashamed. I was embarrassed that I had acted so rashly, and I worried that my missteps reflected poorly on me as a person. It took a while to get through that stage (there's a whole chapter on this later in the book), but when I did, I was able to come back to John 3 and see the rest of that wonderful story. Though the encounter began with a confrontation to Nicodemus's sight, it didn't end there. The conversation was about more than Nicodemus's blindness; it was also about creating a pathway for the transformation of both his soul and his consciousness.

I could feel something shifting inside me during that season, and I kept coming back to the single line that Jesus used to redirect his conversation with Nicodemus as the fodder for change: "Very truly I tell you, no one can see the kingdom of God unless they are born again" (John 3:3).

I reflected on this verse for weeks and months, meditating on its multiple nuances. The first of three words that became transformational for me was simply the word *see.* One of the leadership axioms that I frequently heard at Willow Creek was, "If you want to get the right answer, you have to first ask the right question." I knew I had been asking the wrong question when it came to racial reconciliation and cultural identity.

Each step of my journey to that point had been driven by the question "What am I supposed to do?" But now that question made far too many assumptions about the foundation I was launching from. The far better starting point would have simply been "Can I see?" with the obvious answer being no. That would then lead to the true question of transformation, the question that needed to define my journey from that point forward: "Jesus, will you help me to see?"

The second word in this verse that transformed me was *kingdom*. While *kingdom* represents numerous layers of theological depth, for the purposes of this journey, I saw it as a synonym for *reality*. Jesus was showing Nicodemus that he most needed to *see* that two different realities were colliding. Through his natural eyes, Nicodemus would remain limited as to how much he could see of the world around him. But through eyes that were spiritually reborn by the Spirit, he would see the reality of God in an entirely new fashion.

When I applied this to the realm of race and cultural identity, I could see the same dynamic at play in my life. The kingdom of this world submits to an ordered reality, and if I looked only through my natural eyes, I would be severely limited in how much I could see. But if I allowed my eyes to be spiritually reborn through the Spirit, I could comprehend the full reality of God's kingdom, which would forever change how I thought and acted.

The third and final term that became transformational was *born again*. For many reasons I have come to love this phrase, but at the top of the list is that it is an emphatic declaration that transformation is God's central goal. There's nothing about it that sounds additive or incremental. Instead it paints the picture of a complete reboot. It describes a comprehensive renewal.

If that weren't enough, *born again* also clarifies to whom the realm of transformation belongs: God alone. One of the amazing realities that emerges from this interaction is that nothing was required from Nicodemus other than surrender. When Jesus said that no one could see the kingdom of God unless that person is born again, he didn't expect Nicodemus to bring sight to his own eyes. Sight is the work of God. And when Jesus said that Nicodemus must be born again, that most clearly was not something Nicodemus could control. Only the Spirit of God has the power to bring new life like that.

Richard Rohr, one of my favorite theologians and authors, has been very helpful to me on this point. He founded the Center for Action and Contemplation, and one of its vision statements emphasizes the same progression of principles that we see in John 3: "We need a contemplative mind in order to do compassionate action.[3]"

Rohr writes a lot about the spiritual life beginning with a foundation of contemplation, or what he refers to as a "transformed consciousness." The English word *consciousness* comes from the Latin root *conscire*, which means "to be aware with." Therefore a *transformed* consciousness involves an awareness of the kingdom of God that comes from a revelation of Jesus Christ.

That's exactly what Jesus was getting at in his conversation with Nicodemus. There's a reality that belongs to God alone, and Jesus is the one that ushers us into it. This is a journey he longs to lead us on and a journey we're invited to participate in. But the price of admission is a full acknowledgment of our utter blindness. Only when we embrace our lack of sight can we authorize Jesus to begin the process of illuminating the truth that we so badly need to see.

The transformational metaphor of blindness-to-sight is used throughout the Bible and is applicable to many arenas of the Christian life. In this book, I'm going to rely heavily on this imagery to describe the cultural identity journey.

It is particularly important for white Americans to approach this subject matter with the right goals in mind. Our goal must be sight. Our goal must be transformation. Our goal must be a renewed consciousness.

As such, I urge you to let go of preconceived notions of expertise or understanding that you feel you might be bringing to this.

Instead let's look to Nicodemus as our model.

Let's embrace the reality that, like him, we are stumbling toward Jesus in the dark.

Let's embrace the reality that we don't know the right questions, much less the right answers.

Let's embrace the fact that God's kingdom is at stake and that we need revelation from Jesus Christ in order to see what the kingdom of God is.

Let's enter this journey with new eyes—eyes like a child.

Let's pray like the blind man: "Lord, help me to see."

3

What Is Cultural Identity?

What is cultural identity?

Answering this question requires a common understanding of *identity*, so let's start there. There's an enormous volume of literature addressing this question, and the full range of material is more than I can delve into here. With that being said, many would agree that identity is deeply informed by a pair of questions: "Who am I?" and "How do I fit into the world?"

The answers to these questions lay the foundation of identity throughout childhood. However, children lack the physical and cognitive development needed to reflect deeply on the full meaning of identity until adolescence, when our capacity for self-reflection and self-consciousness deepen.[1] That's when we're able to ask questions like "Who am I?" and "How do I fit into the world?"

With the benefit of hindsight, many of us can see ways in which we experimented with answering identity questions as we progressed toward adulthood. Our teenage years in particular are dominated by attempts to figure out which social category we fit into and where we fall in the hierarchy of our particular social setting.

Like most teens, I was borderline obsessed with finding a sense of identity in my high school years. Like a kid sifting through outfits on the store rack, I tried on each one, desperately hoping to find a fit. In my school, the choices were basically limited to the jock, the brooding artist, the cheerleader, the skater, the Goth kid, the musician, the athlete, the punk rocker, the nerdy but interesting scholar, and the rebel without a cause.

Fortunately, everything changed for me when a new category suddenly emerged. A boy band by the name of New Kids on the Block burst onto the scene, and it was as if I had a revelation. Jordan Knight was the lead singer of NKOTB (yes, you had to use the acronym if you were truly cool), and he was the heartthrob of every teenage girl I knew. So my mission in life was finally clear: I needed to figure out how to become Jordan, and by proxy, to pass as a potential member of a boy band.

My wardrobe began to transform. Sleeveless denim vest? Check. Sports jacket wrapped around my waist? Check. Black button-down shirt with mesh sleeves? Check. The clincher was the silver hoop earring, though. That was Jordan Knight's defining fashion contribution, and I was going to make it mine as well.

I knew this wouldn't be easy, as I was a pastor's kid living in a very conservative Christian environment. Any attempts at putting a hole in my body were going to be met with some Old Testament wrath, so I had to find a nontraditional route. Fortunately (if that's the right word), I had a friend who taught me how to pierce my own ear with a cube of ice. (Hint for anyone considering the same: the ice doesn't really help.) It was a high price to pay for being a self-declared member of a boy band, but I was committed to the course. Therefore I would pierce my ear before every major social event and then pray that the hole would close back up before I got home. What we do to fit into the world!

The story of my manic attempt to fit in as an awkward teenager illustrates the definition of *identity* in this book. Again, our identity is typically shaped by two fundamental questions: "Who am I?" and "How do I fit into the world?" While these questions apply to the formation of individual identity, they are also relevant to the exploration of *cultural* identity.

Before defining *cultural identity*, it might be helpful to explore a couple concepts of *culture*. Sherwood Lingenfelter, a Christian missiologist, notes in his book *Ministering Cross-Culturally* that all human behavior occurs within specific cultures, making it a particularly important idea to engage. Culture shapes the way we order our life, interpret our experiences, and evaluate the behavior of other people.[2] Another take is the popularized definition from Richard Brislin and Tomoko Yoshida: "Culture consists of concepts, values, and assumptions about life that guide behavior and are widely shared by people.... [These] are transmitted generation to generation, rarely with explicit instructions, by parents, teachers, religious figures, and other respected elders."[3]

These two descriptions help us understand the intersection of culture and identity. Brislin and Yoshida first note that culture consists of assumptions that we make; these assumptions are then transmitted from generation to generation. Lingenfelter notes that culture shapes the way we interpret our experiences as well as how we evaluate the behaviors of others. Taken together, I would summarize the most pertinent information regarding cultural identity as this: culture plays a direct and significant role in how we learn to *see* both our neighbors and ourselves. Culture shapes how and what we see, and how and what we see shapes our everyday behaviors and actions.

Therefore, when I use the term *cultural identity* in this book, I define it this way: how a person answers the questions "Who am I?" and "How do I fit into the world?" through the lenses of culture, race, ethnicity, and/or class.

Same Planet — Different Worlds

No writer has had a greater impact on my understanding of cultural identity than Dr. Beverly Tatum. A widely recognized authority on the topic, Tatum has a glittering résumé to underscore her expertise: she was the ninth president of Spelman College (the oldest historically black women's college in the United States) and wrote the best-selling *Why Are All the Black Kids Sitting Together in the Cafeteria?*, an expansive exploration of cultural identity. Tatum now lectures nationally on the connection between cultural identity and educational achievement.

When introducing cultural identity (or racial identity, a term she uses synonymously), Tatum tells a simple but poignant story of two eighth-grade girls, one black and the other white. The story serves as a parable of sorts for the cultural identity journey and reveals how even an everyday encounter can have dramatically different implications on people of different races.[4]

The story begins with a seemingly harmless interaction between a white schoolteacher, Mr. Smith, and the black eighth grader. Mr. Smith is one of the chaperones for the school dance coming up, and he's telling the class how excited he is. He asks the young black woman if she's planning to attend, and she says no. She informs him that the black students are bussed into the mostly white neighborhood, and one of the unfortunate results of this social inequality is their lack of transportation to extracurricular activities. If the event doesn't happen during school hours, there will be no black students in attendance.

Sharing information like this is no small task for the young black woman. The daily commute from her homogeneously black neighborhood into this homogeneously white neighborhood is a constant reminder that she is an "other." She often feels that she is an outsider looking in, and the inability to find transportation to extracurricular events only exasperates this feeling. It was courageous and vulnerable for her to discuss this with the teacher.

Despite the gravity of her statement, Mr. Smith misses its significance. He is fixated on the school dance and is determined to convince this young woman to attend. Ignoring the information she just shared, he does his best to persuade her to reconsider. When he sees that his efforts are failing to yield any change, he mutters one final comment: "Oh come on, I know you people love to dance."

This final line drops like a bomb. While it's unclear to this young woman the full extent of what Mr. Smith meant by it, that doesn't change the sting of the statement. When he included her in the "you people" group, it struck at the heart of one of her deepest suspicions. Though she couldn't prove it, she sensed she was an outsider in Mr. Smith's class. It seemed he treated her differently than the other students, and she feared it could be due to her race. The careless use of "you people" has poured fresh gasoline all over the tinder of her fears.

On the verge of tears, she bursts out of the classroom, and there she serendipitously bumps into her best friend. The friend, who is white, responds immediately with genuine concern. She probes for what made her friend so upset, and the black student decides to recount the entire episode. She reveals that she has often felt like a cultural outsider in Mr. Smith's classroom and shares how his "you people" comment shook her to the core.

Since they have been friends for a while, the black girl assumes that this will be met with empathy and understanding. But to her surprise, the white eighth grader skips right over the feelings of sadness, shock, shame, and anger. Instead she comes to the defense of the teacher, responding, "Oh, Mr. Smith is such a nice guy. I'm sure he didn't mean it like that. Don't be so sensitive."

The young black woman wants to give her friend the benefit of the doubt, but the lack of awareness around what happened is more than she can bear. She realizes that though she loves her friend—and trusts that her friend loves her—it was unwise to share something so delicate in a crosscultural setting. Nursing her wounds from these back-to-back encounters, the young black woman goes to find someone that might understand her pain.

When White Culture Wins

This is a brilliant story for introducing cultural identity because Tatum was able take an everyday occurrence and clearly juxtapose the experience of the black eighth grader with that of the white eighth grader. It wasn't the first time the young black woman had seen something like that. By then she was already familiar with "two-ness"—the experience of operating in one America that's white and one America that's black. W. E. B. Du Bois, the famous sociologist, historian, and civil rights activist, coined the term *double-consciousness* to describe this experience of two-ness. In his seminal book *The Souls of Black Folk*, Du Bois described double-consciousness as the psychological challenge of "always looking at one's self through the eyes" of a white society.[5]

Two-ness is exactly what this young eighth grader was wrestling with as she interacted with the foundational questions of identity: "Who am I?" and "How do I fit in the world?" In some of her circles, these questions were met with affirming voices, and her emerging sense of identity was celebrated and lifted up. But in other circles, she had to reckon with a different story. She was told that there was a different standard for white people than for black people. She was told that she needed to be on high alert in regard to her behaviors and actions whenever she was in all-white spaces. She was told that she needed to perform at a higher level than her white peers if she hoped to overcome prejudices and implicit biases. If she hoped to develop a stable cultural identity, she would have to find a way to reconcile those opposing messages.

If two-ness was the lens by which the black eighth grader viewed this encounter, then what about the white eighth grader? What did she see? Based on her response, the answer is "not much." She certainly didn't see the deeper meaning behind her friend's pain. And if she had any vantage point at all, it was fixed on the need to defend Mr. Smith's motives from being misinterpreted.

So why was the sight of this white eighth grader so limited? Why was she unable to see the deeper meaning behind Mr. Smith's statement?

Let's pause to allow the weight of those questions sink in, because the answers are directly relevant to you and me as well. One aspect of this story should provoke us: while the white eighth grader had sincere *intentions*, it didn't change the fact that the consequences of her actions led to pain for her friend. A lack of vision often places us in the same position: sincere intentions but harmful consequences.

So let's reiterate this important question: Why was the white eighth grader unable to see the deeper meaning of this encounter between her black friend and Mr. Smith? And what does that reveal to us about dimensions of the cultural identity journey that we are often blind to?

I would suggest that first we must contend with the *normalization of white culture*. While that phrase may sound like a mouthful, it reflects a reality that powerfully shapes our daily interactions, so we must look at it carefully.

Let me start with an academic description of the phrase before moving to some everyday illustrations. British sociologist Alistair Bonnet conducted extensive research on white culture in both America and Britain, and he noted that there was something unique about white culture, especially when observed in relation to nonwhite cultures: in both countries white culture is the "norm" by which all other cultural identities are evaluated. White culture is an "unchanging and unproblematic location, a position from which all other identities come to be marked by their difference."[6] In plain language, he said that when we attempt to categorize culture internally, we almost always treat white cultural as "normal." With white culture serving as the baseline, we then evaluate everyone else's culture based on the norms we associate with white culture.

I took a seminary class with a white, racially conscious professor years ago, and he was convinced of this hypothesis. He regularly challenged his students to engage in self-examination of what we assumed to be culturally "normal" and illustrated the prevalence of white normalization in as many ways as possible. During one class, he pulled out a census form to make his point, and asked, "Have you ever noticed how every cultural group on the census is defined in proximity to white Americans? You have Native American, African American, Asian American, Latino/a American, and so on. What is *not* overtly stated is how normalized *white* American culture is. All of these identities are labeled relative to the location of white culture."

He would then urge his students to consider the way the normalization of whiteness also revealed itself through everyday vocabulary. He asked, "Have you ever heard a person's first name described as 'weird' or 'unusual'? White people calling it weird or unusual don't necessarily mean to overtly appeal to race; yet that's almost always what they mean.

"Many names are considered 'normal' within white culture, and when a name is seen as weird or unusual, it's usually because the name doesn't fall within that standard. The same is true when we describe an individual's personal fashion as 'weird' or 'unusual.' It's weird or unusual in comparison to the white default."

Since these were all seminary students, he delighted in showing us the way this normalization of whiteness was reflected in our own institution. He said, "Each of you will be required to take a handful of core theology classes before you graduate. That's good—you should. But I want to show you something interesting." He powered up the projector and brought an online catalog of classes up on the screen. "Watch this," he said. "There are core, required classes that are just called theology. But when you go to the electives, you will see that, in the spirit of diversity, we offer an array of additional theology classes: black theology, Latin theology, Asian theology, etc. A question begs to be asked: Why do all of those theology classes have a modifier before them? Where is the category of white theology? I will answer it for you: you won't find one. The theology passed on to us from white forefathers is considered to be the normal, default standard for theology. It is the assumed cultural norm. Everyone else's theology is defined in relation to whiteness."

In time I began to see how this was far more than a theoretical exercise. The normalization of white culture dramatically affects cultural identity development, and both white people and people of color feel its effects.

Consider my friend Samuel as example of this effect. He was raised by a white father and Chinese American mother, and they lived in a wealthy suburb just outside of Chicago. Despite living in a mixed-race home, Samuel never thought much about race or culture growing up.

When he was twelve, that began to change. He had been in the same elementary school from grades pre-K through sixth grade, so his friendship circle had remained steady during those years. When seventh grade came, everyone went to different junior high schools, and with that came the prospect of having to form new friendships. Samuel felt nervous, as all young students do when moving into new circles. But with a naturally outgoing personality, he figured he'd be able to make new friends easily.

When he began attending classes at the new school, which was predominantly white, he was bombarded with a new question—one he had never been asked before: "What are you?"

In some ways, that question could be interpreted as innocent and even expected from adolescents. Samuel's peers were engaging in identity development in a more thorough way than they had in their childhood years, and with increased enlightenment came new levels of curiosity. But at another level, we expect this question from any young person growing up in a society that normalizes white culture. These seventh graders had never taken a class on being white. They had never been explicitly indoctrinated about what is acceptable in white culture and what is not. And yet, by the time they were twelve, they had developed a keen sense of what is considered culturally "normal." They had inherited a racial classification system that normalized whiteness, and based on that, were attempting to categorize Samuel. This "what are you?" question wasn't just in the bad manners category; it was in the "I'm measuring you against my culturally normal" category.

Let me tell one last story, with the hope of driving home the relationship between cultural identity and the normalization of white culture. I recognize that mentioning politics may pull unnecessary triggers, but I bring it up to raise a point about race and culture, not about politics. In November 2016, Donald Trump was elected to be the next president of the United States, and the aftermath sent shock waves along racial lines through the American church. Though it isn't unusual for Christians to fall on separate sides of the political spectrum, there was something unique about Trump's campaign. A majority of Christians of color viewed the rhetoric that marked his run for president as racist, sexist, and xenophobic, and they felt it was a matter of moral conscience to stand against his campaign in a spirit of resistance. Their assumption was that their white counterparts held to this conviction as well, but the election results told a different story. Eighty-one became a regularly referred-to percentage of white evangelicals who voted for Trump.

The already-present racial divide in the church became further enflamed by the election, and it manifested in some concrete ways. That divide was on display in the betrayal and anger many Christians of color communicated toward white Christians. Some of the respected bridge-building leaders went so far as to publicly question whether there could ever be genuine unity across racial lines in the American church.

On the other side were white Christians, many of them displaying shock at the outrage from their brothers and sisters of color. To them the election was about something very different from race, and they were perplexed about why the results had landed so hard on people of color. What became clear to everyone during this time was that regardless of where one's political views landed, the result was that the racial breach between Christians had grown qualitatively worse.

Social media was the universe in which conversations on race ignited. It seemed that I was pulled into an intensely charged conversation daily during that era, and one in particular elucidates the intersection between cultural identity and the normalization of whiteness. It happened on one of my social media pages and involved three friends with whom I had worked closely in a previous ministry setting. Two of them were white, and they were part of a group that was attempting to understand why people of color felt so betrayed by the election. The third friend was a man of Filipino descent (I will call him Jonathan), who was doing his best to engage in a way that might help them understand the collective heartache.

The conversation began at a theoretical level as the three of them volleyed political ideas back and forth. But the disposition of the conversation quickly changed when Jonathan shared that the pain he was feeling was not tied to political differences or partisan alliances. He said,

> This has nothing to do with Republicans or Democrats. I love America. I grew up in this country. I appreciate the democracy we have, and typically I don't care much about whom my friends vote for, as long as they vote their conscience. But this election was different. This election changed my daily reality. For the first time in my life, I am waking up every morning scared. I feel like the tenor of this election gave those with hate in their hearts permission to speak it out loud—maybe to even act on it. I feel like I don't know whom I can trust anymore, and I am anxious all of the time. That's the bottom line—as a person of color, I feel genuinely scared. That is what I wish you guys would see and understand.

This was a courageous thing to share, and I was moved by his words. It was an act of vulnerability, and I found myself praying that the three of us white friends would have the eyes to see what he was sharing.

William, the most outspoken in this dialogue, was the first to respond. His initial words gave me hope that he was indeed beginning to see things in a new way: "Wow, Jonathan, thank you for sharing that. I had no idea you felt so scared. I am really sorry that this is your experience." But then he added,

> I can't believe you said you are a person of color though. Are you really a person of color? You and I have been friends for years, and I have never heard you say that. Why are you all of sudden saying things like that? I would be cautious to talk about race too much right now—that's not going to help any of our situations. I really don't think you have anything to worry about. I've never once thought of you as any different than me, and I'm sure nobody else will see you any different either. You are going to be fine bro—just trust in God.

My heart sank when I read these words. I had known William for a number of years, and I trusted that the motives behind his misguided attempt at comforting Jonathan were sincere. But I could also see how William had just embodied unprocessed, normalized whiteness. As a highly educated, white man, he had never felt the danger that comes with being seen as the racial or cultural "other." All he'd ever known was being culturally "normal." This made it exceedingly difficult for him to empathize with the daily risks that Jonathan was facing in this climate, and it placed a limit on his ability to be a good and faithful friend in that moment.

Furthermore, William's response showed that he did have some idea of how powerful white culture is. By letting Jonathan know "I've never once thought of you as any different than _me_" and then reassuring him that "nobody else will see you any different either," he was making a direct appeal to race and culture. His logic was likely formed at a subconscious level, but he was nonetheless basing his reassurance on Jonathan's proximity to whiteness. And though my translation may come across as more direct than what William said, the logic of what he was arguing sounded something like this: "Jonathan, there is nothing for you to be afraid of. When I see you, I don't see a Filipino man. I see someone white, or at least acceptable to whites. I am confident that other white people will see you like this as well. So don't worry anymore—you are all good."

I don't tell this story to disparage William. To be white and to step into unchartered waters around race and culture is to guarantee that moments like this will arise in each of our journeys. If we place too much emphasis on being politically correct or on the hope of avoiding mistakes, we miss the chance to learn humbly from moments of revelation.

I hope this story and the others explored here bring into sharp focus the point of this section: each of us who are serious about a deep and authentic engagement with cultural identity need to contend with *the normalization of white culture*. No person is exempt.

As for the hope of staying strong on this journey, I believe it's helpful to name a couple of the tensions felt by white people and contending with the normalization of whiteness. For one, we confront the confusion that comes with trying to describe what has always been normal to us. Though a white person could clearly be an outsider in another social category (such as gender, religion, sexual orientation, age, or physical or mental ability), it isn't possible to be a cultural outsider when it comes to race. When the time comes for us to engage whiteness, we feel disoriented, because we aren't practiced at it.

A metaphor I've heard to describe this confusion is that of fish trying to analyze the water they live in; they're surrounded by it, and it's impossible to see. I would take it even further: If you take a fish out of the water, it immediately gasps for air and does whatever it can to stay alive. Though there's no reason for a human being to view the cultural identity journey in as dramatic of terms as a fish out of water, my experience suggests that this is what it often feels like for white people. There are moments when it feels so uncomfortable we gasp for air.

That leads to a second tension that white people must learn to manage when contending with the normalization of whiteness: privilege. *Privilege* can be a loaded word, but to simplify it for the journey of cultural identity, I appeal to the definition of Rev. Julian DeShazier. Julian is a pastor who does a lot of great work with racial reconciliation in the Hyde Park neighborhood of Chicago and is also known as the successful hip-hop artist J. Kwest. One of the concepts he frequently talks about in crosscultural settings is privilege, which he simply defines as "the ability to walk away."

This is one of the essential truths we as white people need to remember (or become aware of, if it's new) as we contend with the normalization of whiteness. When the journey begins to feel like any combination of scary, confusing, disorienting, or even painful, we have a privilege that people of color do not: we can walk away; we can go back to "normal," if we choose.

Christians and Cultural Identity

Before wrapping up our exploration of cultural identity, let's look at a couple of important conversation points that are distinct to the Christian journey. In the last chapter I shared some of the story of my unsuccessful attempt to start a culturally diverse ministry in the city of Chicago (Metro 212). There were many lessons that I learned during that era, but the need to have a theologically informed approach to cultural identity was at the top of the list. I would eventually go on to plant a new faith community called River City Community Church (a name inspired by Revelation 22:1-4) in Chicago with a group of people in January 2003, and this time we were ready to integrate the need for cultural identity development into our overall understanding of Christian discipleship.

It is worth noting that the dynamics that come with the cultural identity journey shift as you work with individuals of diverse cultural backgrounds, and that must certainly be taken into account for anyone leading in a multicultural context. Since the focus of this book is exclusively on the cultural identity journey of white people, I would like to address some of the specific dynamics that tend to arise for those of us who are white.

I have worked with hundreds of white Christians over the years at River City who are actively seeking to deepen their understanding of cultural identity. I also have had the opportunity to engage with white Christians on this topic in a variety of contexts, including groups ranging from pastors to college students and social settings ranging from rural to suburban to urban. While each of those environments creates a different backdrop for the conversation, I consistently find that the questions, objections, and sticking points remain remarkably similar. Much of what I've learned from these conversations will be shared in the next few chapters. For now, here are two themes that have become foundational for my conversations in these groups and that need to be mentioned in this chapter on cultural identity:

- ◆ The Bible provides a unique motivation for Christians to engage with cultural identity.

- ◆ A cultural identity blind spot within white Christian circles undermines the entire process when left unaddressed.

The biblical motivation for engaging in cultural identity. One of the distinctive traits of Christianity is a commitment to God's revelation of truth in Scripture, so that should be the starting point for a Christ follower's journey toward cultural identity. While there is much worth saying about the theology of cultural identity, I typically begin by focusing on the material throughout Scripture that emphasizes the centrality of *identity transformation*. Consider as a small sample some of the foundational terms and concepts from the Christian vocabulary and the way they highlight identity transformation.

Born again. We explored this phrase in the last chapter, and it's one of the most comprehensive identity terms in the Bible. Being born again requires recognition that one can't become a mature Christian by just attending a class, reading a book, or doing good deeds. Instead there must be a complete overhaul of how we understand our identity. Like a baby entering the world for the first time, we enter into a new way of life in Christ. The deep-water questions of identity—"Who am I?" and "How do I fit into the world?"—are now to be answered exclusively through our new status in Christ.

Baptized. As the sacrament most closely associated with Christian conversion, baptism is saturated with the language of identity transformation. To be baptized is to make the decision (or have your parents make it for you) to be permanently and eternally identified with the person of Jesus Christ. Even more importantly, to be baptized is to accept the gift of having God identify with us. When Jesus got baptized, God the Father affirmed the precious gift of belovedness: "This is my son, whom I love; with him I am well pleased" (Matthew 3:17).

Child of God. In Romans 8:14-17, the apostle Paul points us to the mystical reality that through the Spirit of God we have been adopted as sons and daughters, and therefore we are now heirs of God and coheirs with Christ. Everything we do is to be informed by this reality; our family relations now shape our identity. We are to take on the character of Christ (our older brother) and to pursue what is core to the heart of God (our heavenly Father).

Disciple of Christ. Translated most frequently as a *learner* or *student*, a disciple is someone whose identity is now fully defined by his or her relationship to the master Rabbi. Our will, our attitude, and our behaviors are then all informed by our identity in Christ. The word *Christian* is virtually synonymous to this, as those who were outside the faith created and applied the term to those whose identity was then wrapped up in the person of Jesus (Acts 11:26; 26:28).

Theology is one of my greatest passions, and I particularly enjoy studying what the Bible says about this topic. For the purpose of this chapter, and for the overall defining of cultural identity, let me simply emphasize this: the Bible provides us with a unique and powerful motivation for pursuing wholesale, identity transformation in Christ.

Identity transformation doesn't happen in a vacuum. It requires honesty, reflection, and acknowledgement of the significant forces that have helped shape who we were prior to devoting our lives to Christ as well as who we are moving forward. Because culture plays such a major role in shaping our identity, Christian discipleship requires us to engage deeply with cultural identity as well.

The Blind Spot That Undermines the Process

Though the Bible presents us with a unique motivation for pursuing cultural identity, we're immediately at risk of having that motivation undercut by a persistent misconception within many Christian circles: *colorblindness*. Religious people don't have a monopoly on colorblindness, as there are people of every background who have it. Colorblindness minimizes the racial-cultural heritage of a person and promotes a culturally neutral approach that sees people independent of their heritage.

Though you can find the presence of colorblind ideology in all sectors of society, a uniquely powerful version is circulating in the Christian context. The ideology of Christian colorblindness is fortified by theological truths that are unfortunately misapplied to cultural identity. The short form usually sounds something like this: "God did not create multiple races; there is just one race: humankind." As human beings, we share more in common than difference. We have all sinned, we are all in need of redemption, we are all equals at the foot of the cross, and through faith we are all one in Christ.

Every part of that sentence is theologically accurate; sin, salvation, and redemption are equally applicable to people of every race and creed. The problem is that those same truths are incorrectly applied to cultural identity, leaving us with a dangerous form of colorblindness. Consider just a handful of reasons why colorblindness is a dangerous ideology for Christians to subscribe to and why it can thwart authentic engagement with cultural identity.

Colorblindness minimizes the role cultural identity played in the story of many Old Testament heroes. Once you begin to view the Bible through a lens that includes cultural identity, you discover the major role it played in the mission of so many of the "cloud of witnesses" (Hebrews 12:1).

- Joseph was born a Jew but emerged as the second most powerful man in Egypt next to Pharaoh.

- Moses was the greatest leader of his time, and the crucible of his leadership development was in being caught between his Jewish ancestry and his Egyptian upbringing.

- God lifted up Esther as a leader to prevent Jewish genocide, but that happened only after Mordecai challenged her to remember her cultural roots.

- Ruth's account repeatedly notes that her cultural background was that of a Moabite, and it became a major theme in her redemption story.

- Daniel was a Jewish boy brought into Babylonian captivity, and his depth of maturity allowed him to navigate his cultural identity in legendary ways. He is revered for his devotion to the God of the Torah, yet he also received a Babylonian name (Belteshazzar) as he rose up the ranks of their government.

Colorblindness minimizes the incarnation of Christ. As theologically significant as it is that God incarnated into humankind, we must be careful not to miss that Jesus came to earth embodied within a specific cultural identity. While he transcends skin color and racial divisions, Jesus the human being was a Jew, and one who most likely had somewhat dark skin.

Jesus was also born within a specific genealogical line that was culturally significant, and that established him as the son of David (Matthew 1:1). He was a Jewish boy who learned the customs and norms of his culture growing up: he worshiped in synagogues and observed the annual Passover and other feasts in the temple in Jerusalem. He was a Jewish adult whose mastery of the Scriptures in his local synagogue earned him a title of respect: *rabbi*. He was regularly seen and recognized as a Jew from both outside of his culture (such as the Samaritan woman in John 4) and within (at multiple points both his disciples and Jewish leaders reminded him of cultural obligations, ranging from Sabbath observance to ritual washings). Just before Jesus' death, Pilate had inscribed over his head the words "King of the Jews." To be colorblind would be to risk missing some of the deepest meanings of Christ's incarnation.

Colorblindness minimizes the overtones of cultural identity throughout the early church. In Matthew 28:19, Jesus sent his apostles to "go and make disciples of all nations [*ethnos*]," and their endeavors are recorded in the book of Acts. From the very start, we see cultural identity manifesting as a critical dimension of the church:

- In Acts 2, a multicultural gathering became the firewood in which Pentecost was kindled.

- In Acts 6—the first conflict in the early church—we see Grecian widows complaining of being ignored in favor of the dominant cultural group (which then became the genesis of the deacon ministry).

- In Acts 8, we see a pair of cultural breakthroughs: the response of Samaria and then of the Ethiopian eunuch to the gospel.

◆ In Acts 10, the apostle Peter had a vision in which he was confronted about his Jewish-centric view, and he finally realized that the gospel is for Gentiles as well.

◆ And then, in Acts 13, we're introduced to the culturally diverse leadership team that oversaw the church of Antioch—the same church that would become the sending agency for the next generation of congregations. Since this is the only church leadership team named in the Bible, we discover that the early congregations of the New Testament were anything but colorblind.

Colorblindness minimizes the ways God recognizes and celebrates cultural diversity. In Revelation 7:9, we get a glimpse of heaven, and in this glimpse we see a culturally diverse group of people worshiping Christ. This affirms that even in heaven, colorblindness is not an option. Then, in Revelation 21, we see that in the eternal city of God our final state will be enriched because "the kings of the earth will bring their splendor into it" and "the glory and honor of the nations will be brought into it" (vv. 24, 26). God recognizes that different cultures reflect different honors and gifts, and these gifts are for the glory of God.

Each of those four points gives a strong theological case for eliminating Christian colorblindness, but let me finish with the most important of all: *sin*. Christians of every background agree that there is a need to account for the reality of sin. Our "old self" was ruled by sin, and Jesus' death and resurrection both atone for that sin and lead us into a new, resurrected life (Romans 6:5-11). The ongoing work of Christian growth is to pursue redeemed life in God and to participate in the life of Christ in such a way that we no longer allow sin to reign the way it did in our old self (Romans 6:12-14). Therefore, to move forward with Christ means to acknowledge the power of sin. We must name it, confess it, and do all that we can to break free of its former power.

Christian colorblindness is dangerous for many reasons, but the power of sin is at the top of the list. The system of race that we've created in America is fraught with sin, and it has played a powerful role in shaping the sense of identity of every human being who has lived here. Therefore it would be naive for devoted followers of Jesus to believe they can pursue the transformation of identity in Christ without also acknowledging the power of sin as evidenced by the impact of race. Our old self has been profoundly shaped by race, and we can't grow into the new and redeemed self without naming the presence of that sin, confessing the ways it has impacted us, and doing all we can to break free of its former power.

That's why I believe that choosing to remain colorblind is willful ignorance. We would never tolerate a form of Christianity that minimizes sin as it relates to conversion or discipleship; we should therefore never tolerate Christian colorblindness either.

Moving Forward

Most of what shapes our initial sense of identity is beyond our control because it includes our time in history, our families of origin, our gender, and our cultural heritage. But in the human journey, we are able to make choices and to alter our future reality. We can choose to engage in self-reflection. We can choose to engage in theological reflection. We can choose to expose ourselves to perspectives outside our comfort level. We can choose to pursue growth, knowledge, and transformation. When we do, we participate with Christ, who declared, "The old has gone, the new is here!" (2 Corinthians 5:17).

Encounter

Whenever I lead a training session on cultural identity—particularly
when there's a strong white presence—I begin with this question:
"Describe the first encounter you remember having with race." Most
participants answer this with relative ease, and what they share is
always enlightening. In the most recent training I conducted, their
answers included a typical gamut of stories.

The first participant described a crosscultural friendship. A Pakistani family moved into his neighborhood during his elementary
school years, including a boy his age with whom he became fast
friends. He visited his Pakistani friend's home and came into contact
with a range of culturally different practices. The food they ate, the
clothes they wore, and the family dialect stood in contrast to the cultural norms of his white family.

The second participant described the first time she saw a person of
color in a public position of influence, an African American pastor
that spoke at her church. As a seventh grader, she noticed not only the
pastor's unique rhetorical style but also that there was not a single
black person in her own congregation.

The third participant described witnessing an overt act of prejudice,
which is the most common racial encounter white people share with

me. He was walking home from high school with a black friend during his freshman year when a police car followed them from a distance for a couple of blocks before pulling up next to them. The officer rolled down his window and asked the white teenager if everything was all right. He was confused by the question and assured the officer everything was fine. As the police car drove away, he asked his black friend if he had any idea what that was about. The black friend then told him about racial profiling, saying that instances like that were not uncommon for him. This shook the white friend to the core.

This exercise is an important introduction to conversations around race and cultural identity for a couple of reasons. First, it helps participants to reflect on encounters with race that have shaped their understanding. Second, and most important, it serves as a reminder of the normalization of whiteness.

My own story is no different. The first time I was asked to describe my initial encounter with race, my answer came quickly. I was in fifth grade, and my family lived in an all-white neighborhood—until a brave black family moved in. They were there less than a week before someone set fire to a cross in their front yard. I will never forget my confusion and the rage that boiled within me as my father explained the legacy of the Ku Klux Klan to me.

Encounters like these play an important role in the growing consciousness of white Americans, but they must also remind us of how pervasive and normalized white culture is[What about the all-white (or *almost* all-white) neighborhoods we grew up in? Was there a reason they were all white? What about the all-white (or *almost* all-white) roster of teachers we sat under? Was there a reason they were all white? What about the all-white casts we saw on television growing up? Did these not play a role in shaping our views on race and culture? Do these also qualify as encounters with race?]

The answer is obviously yes; we have encountered race daily since the day we were born. But we're taught to internalize white culture as normal, so we're unaware of the profound ways race shaped us during our early years. Not until we have an *interruption* connected to a person of color or a confrontation with overt racism do we begin to see something outside our cultural norm.

So encounter is the first stage of our cultural identity journey. If we are to be liberated from blindness and to move toward greater levels of awakening, we must find a way to see the deeper meaning behind our daily encounters with race. This chapter is about to take a dive into that deeper meaning, but I'd like to share a couple of thoughts first.

This book is built on seven stages (each with its own chapter) that mark the cultural identity process of a white person seeking transformation from blindness to sight: encounter, denial, disorientation, shame, self-righteousness, awakening, and active participation. The six stages after this chapter, "Encounter," can happen in any order. Often a person enters and reenters certain stages at multiple points along the way. But the one stage that remains foundational throughout the process is the encounter. We must learn to see critical encounters with race; if we don't, the rest of the process collapses.

Second, much of the material I'm about to cover in this chapter may be difficult to hear. It isn't easy to ask critical questions about our country's origins or about our own family tree. There may be points in this chapter where you feel I'm being unnecessarily confrontational. You may feel frustrated, defensive, or angry—or sad, defeated, or overwhelmed. If and when you do, I hope that you will see it as an opportunity to embrace the tension, discomfort, and uneasy feelings. Transformation rarely comes easily.

With those two disclaimers in place, let me ask a couple of questions: When we have encounters with race, what should those encounters ignite in us? If we learn to awaken to the racial realities behind encounters, what may we come to see?

The answers to these questions are found in four interlocking racial realities in America. Only when we see these four can we better understand our own cultural identity:

- the social construct of race
- the history of white superiority
- the narrative of racial difference
- the infected social systems

The Social Construct of Race

In chapter one, I shared how my South Asian friend upended my understanding of race when he said, "Daniel, you may be white, but don't let that lull you into thinking you have no culture. White culture is very real. In fact, when white culture comes in contact with other cultures, it almost always wins. So it would be a really good idea for you to learn about your culture." It took me years to understand what he was saying, and not until I began to engage with the American history of race did the fog begin to lift. A helpful starting point for me was learning to distinguish between two words that seem to have similar meanings but are actually very different things: *ethnicity* and *race*.

Ethnicity refers to the way people identify with each other based on commonalities such as language, history, ancestry, nationality, customs, cuisine, and art. Within the larger framework of "white," we can easily identify dozens of ethnicities. I've already mentioned my Irish roots with its customs, language, music, dance, sports, cuisine, and mythology, as well as my German and French heritage. While I haven't immersed myself in those two cultures to the degree that I have my Irish side, examining them has helped me understand ethnicity.

Race is different. There is near unanimous scientific agreement that race is a social construct (that is, it is created by human beings, not God) that goes far beyond the scope of what *ethnicity* describes. Here's how this developed: When Europeans first colonized America, the concept of race, as we know it, did not yet exist. The white people who settled here over the years weren't yet considered white; they were British, French, German, Welsh, Dutch, Italian, Irish, and so on. In fact, they represented a wide range of cultural, ethnic, and economic differences, and the idea of viewing them through a single racial lens would have been outlandish.

That began to change when slavery became an integral part of the American fabric. The economic machine created by Europeans was expanding at a torrid pace, and its dark secret was its reliance on slave labor as its primary fuel. The horror of slavery was a major moral crisis for America, but instead of acknowledging the sin of that enterprise, we went in the opposite direction. We began to deemphasize the differences within various European ethnicities and began to describe white people as a human collective that was inherently superior to people of color.

In his critically acclaimed book *The Wages of Whiteness*, David Roediger, a professor of American studies and history at Kansas University, made the case that slavery had a dramatic impact on the social construction of race and specifically on what we now consider to be *white*. He contended that this construct was a conscious effort by slave owners to gain distance from those they enslaved. Though there had been no collective sense of *white* before slavery, that changed quickly. By the eighteenth century, Roediger wrote, *white* had become well established as a racial term in the United States. By the end of the nineteenth century, it had become an all-encompassing term.[1]

Another book often cited when exploring the social construct of race is Noel Ignatiev's *How the Irish Became White*. Ignatiev tracked the historical immigration patterns of the Irish to America and contended that in their early years here, they were mistreated, oppressed, and seen as inferior to other European ethnic groups. Ignatiev wrote that because of their suffering, they formed a unique bond with

African Americans: they lived side by side, they shared workspaces, and they were part of the same class competing for the same jobs. When the census was taken in 1850, the term *mulatto* was introduced for the first time and used primarily to describe a person of both Irish and African American descent.

The Irish immigration overlapped with the continued development of the social construct of race, and a powerful white republic was emerging. Ignatiev suggested that due to their desire to be accepted as white, the Irish embraced racism against American blacks and supported the institution of slavery. As they began to achieve acceptance into the white race, some Irish embraced an even more virulent strain of racism that emphasized their differences from blacks. In essence, the Irish became white, helping to solidify the modern concept of the white race.

The History of White Supremacy

For many of us the term *white supremacy* evokes strong images ranging from the Ku Klux Klan to the Nazi regime. When we get past the emotional response to the term and consider its definition, we can see that it remains relevant. According to Dictionary.com, *white supremacy* is "the belief, theory, or doctrine that white people are inherently superior to people from all other racial groups, especially black people, and are therefore rightfully the dominant group in any society."[2]

Race is a social construct, as explored earlier, and white supremacy is an ideology (or belief, theory, or doctrine) that has informed and sustained this construct. Said another way, the system of race in America has consistently treated white people as a superior race and has consistently treated nonwhites as inferior.

While this can be difficult to hear, it isn't difficult to prove. Let's begin with the Declaration of Independence, the document that established our nation. One of the most appealing things about it is the way it articulates these fundamental ideas: "We hold these Truths to be self-evident, that all Men are created equal, that they are endowed by their Creator with certain unalienable Rights, that among these are Life, Liberty, and the Pursuit of Happiness."

While this was a brave and noble vision (at least for men—it did not include women), the description of people indigenous to the land was neither brave nor noble: "The Inhabitants of our Frontiers, *the merciless Indian Savages*, whose known Rule of Warfare, is an undistinguished Destruction, of all Ages, Sexes and Conditions."[3]

Our definition of white supremacy is key at this point, because it stresses the belief (or doctrine) not only that white people are inherently superior but also that they are *rightfully* the dominant group. The creation account in Genesis highlights one of the ways human dominance is exerted: "Now the LORD God had formed out of the ground all the wild animals and all the birds in the sky. He brought them to the man to see what he would name them; and whatever the man called each living creature, that was its name" (Genesis 2:19).

When Adam named the lesser members of creation in the Garden of Eden, he was exercising dominance in the literal sense: in Genesis 1:28, God gave humankind dominion over the fish in the sea, the birds in the sky, and every living creature that moves on the ground. It was an exercise in power that approached divine-like levels, and it was a power that was to be stewarded with extreme caution.

The founders accepted a distorted version of the dominion that God entrusted to Adam and Eve in the Garden of Eden. But this form of dominion was *especially* sinful. Not only did they anoint us with a power that was not ours, they also used it to name other human beings.

If this weren't audacious enough, they went beyond just naming in a generic way: they chose to found our country on a dehumanizing picture of an entire group of people being fundamentally "merciless" and "savage." The Bible repetitively refers to human beings as God's treasured possession, and to dehumanize another person is to demean those who are valuable according to God.

The act of encoding white supremacy into foundational documents did not end with the Declaration. It's splashed across the pages of the US Constitution as well. Written during the height of slavery in America, article 1, section 2, paragraph 3 says this about people of African descent:

> Representatives and direct Taxes shall be apportioned among the several States which may be included within this Union, according to their respective Numbers, which shall be determined by adding to the whole Number of free Persons, including those bound to Service for a Term of Years, and excluding Indians not taxed, *three fifths of all other Persons*.[4]

When they referred to African Americans as three-fifths human in this Constitutional provision, they literally dehumanized a group of people in the fullest sense of the word. This mathematical equation demonstrated how the racial hierarchy was viewed: white people were 100 percent human, but black people were only three-fifths.

Some defendants of the Constitution contend that it's unfair to use the three-fifths human clause as an example of inferiority because that was just a tactic used to negotiate the tax system. But arguing that point suggests that this provision is the only place where we see the historical dichotomy between black life and white life. Another unsightly example is the social and legal principle referred to as the one-drop rule: any person with even one drop of sub-Saharan African blood was to be considered black. The message sent through this law and others like it was clear: whites were the superior race, and even a single drop of inferior blood contaminated the purity of whiteness.

Though white supremacy was aimed at native and black people in a unique and devastating way, it was also the foundation of how we named and depicted other groups of color. For instance, in his book *Mongrels, Bastards, Orphans, and Vagabonds*, Gregory Rodriguez traced the way the dehumanizing word *mongrel* was used to paint

Mexican people. In the 1850s, at the time of the conquest of the Southwest, Secretary of State James Buchanan, who also served as the fifteenth US president, warned white Americans of the dangers of hosting a "mongrel race."[5] In the 1920s, Representative John C. Box warned that allowing immigration would lead to the "distressing process of mongrelization" in America.[6] And in more recent memory, Donald Trump took this narrative further in his 2015 presidential campaign, saying, "When Mexico sends its people, they're not sending their best. . . . They're bringing drugs. They're bringing crime. They're rapists."[7]

Ronald Takaki, author of *A Different Mirror: A History of Multicultural America*, demonstrated ways that the Chinese experienced white supremacy as well. At the California constitutional convention of 1878, John F. Miller warned, "Were the Chinese to amalgamate at all with our people, it would be the lowest, most vile and degraded of our race, and the result of that amalgamation would be a hybrid of the most despicable, a mongrel of the most detestable that has ever afflicted the earth."[8] Two years later, this culminated in laws prohibiting marriage between a white person and a "negro, mulatto, or Mongolian."[9]

In their work on Asian pan-ethnicity, social scientists Kenyon Chan and Shirley Hune explored ways in which other Asian immigrant groups were targeted by the dominant culture. The Japanese and Koreans were regularly referred to as "the yellow peril." Filipinos were derogatorily referred to as "little brown monkeys." Asian Indians, most of them Sikhs, were called "ragheads."[10]

Dr. Eduardo Bonilla-Silva, a professor of sociology at Duke University, poignantly demonstrates how the doctrine of white supremacy has undercut our aspiration of being a nation of equality. He writes of the ways in which the metaphorical "melting pot"—the notion that people of different cultures can mix and melt together into a big cultural pot that is harmonious and happy—was consistently used to promote the vision of equal access to the American dream. He noted that, as appealing as this vision is, it was never possible. Because our culture asserts that white people are superior, people of color never have equal access to that pot. In a PBS documentary on race, Bonilla-Silva memorably said it like this: "[The] melting pot never included people of color. Blacks, Chinese, Puerto Ricans, etcetera, could not melt into the pot. They could be used as wood to produce the fire for the pot, but they could not be used as material to be melted into the pot."[11]

wow.

The Narrative of Racial Difference

I will use the phrase *narrative of racial difference* from this point forward, because it has been a very helpful tool for my own navigation through cultural identity and that of other white folks. Bryan Stevenson was the first to popularize this terminology. He is a nationally recognized lawyer that has dedicated his career to helping the poor, the incarcerated, and the condemned, and he is one of the great activists of our day.[12]

Stevenson is a brilliant thinker on race, and the linchpin of his ideas is the narrative of racial difference. Here's how he described it in an interview:

> The whole narrative of white supremacy was created during the era of slavery. It was a necessary theory to make white Christian people feel comfortable with their ownership of other human beings. And we created a narrative of racial difference in this country to sustain slavery, and even people who didn't own slaves bought into that narrative, including people in the North. . . . So this narrative of racial difference has done really destructive things in our society. Lots of countries had slaves, but they were mostly societies with slaves. We became something different, we became a slave society. We created a narrative of racial difference to maintain slavery. And our 13th amendment never dealt with that narrative. It didn't talk about white supremacy. The Emancipation

Proclamation doesn't discuss the ideology of white supremacy or the narrative of racial difference, so I don't believe slavery ended in 1865, I believe it just evolved. It turned into decades of racial hierarchy that was violently enforced—from the end of reconstruction until WWII—through acts of racial terror. And in the north, that was tolerated.

And so we are very confused when we start talking about race in this country because we think that things are "of the past" because we don't understand what these things really are, that narrative of racial difference that was created during slavery that resulted in terrorism and lynching, that humiliated, belittled and burdened African Americans throughout most of the 20th century. The same narrative of racial difference that got Michael Brown killed, got Eric Garner killed and got Tamir Rice killed. That got these thousands of others—of African Americans—wrongly accused, convicted and condemned. It is the same narrative that has denied opportunities and fair treatment to millions of people of color, and it is the same narrative that supported and led to the executions in Charleston [South Carolina].[13]

As we reflect on the significance of his description of the narrative of racial difference, let's focus on three of his points.

1. *"We created a narrative of racial difference . . . to maintain slavery."* This connecting back to the first point of this chapter: race in America is a social construct. Taking a different angle than any we've explored, Stevenson points out that early white Christians faced a moral dilemma when it came to slavery: How could they justify the possession and ownership of fellow human beings? He suggests that the only way was to subscribe to a narrative that claimed white people were inherently more human than black people.

2. *"I don't believe slavery ended in 1865, I believe it just evolved."* Here Stevenson observes the difference between the *institution* of slavery

and the *narrative* that undergirded it. The institution was technically overturned on December 6, 1865, when the Thirteenth Amendment to the Constitution was ratified. As important as the legal dismantling of slavery was, it failed to uproot the ideology that allowed it to thrive. If you've ever tried to maintain a garden, you know that uprooting is an important task. You can remove weeds all day, but if the roots aren't extracted, it's just a matter of time before the weeds return.

3. *"It is the same narrative that has denied opportunities and fair treatment to millions of people of color, and it is the same narrative that supported and led to the executions in Charleston."* Here Stevenson challenges us to see the presence of the narrative in the early days of America and to follow the thread throughout the different eras of American history: During slave days, the narrative poisoned our minds to justify owning other human beings. In the late 1800s, it poisoned our minds to participate in lynchings and to watch as people of color (mostly black) were executed publicly without a legal trial. In the mid-1900s, it poisoned our minds to enact Jim Crow laws and to watch as whites-only spaces were built and preserved throughout society. In the later 1900s, it poisoned our minds to criminalize young men of color and establish America as the country with the highest incarceration rate on the planet. In the present, the narrative has produced endless tragedies, including the deaths of Michael Brown, Rekia Boyd, Eric Garner, Sandra Bland, Tamir Rice, and many more.

This quote from Stevenson is useful on multiple levels. First, the *narrative of racial difference* integrates the two racial realities we covered in this chapter: race is a social construct, and this construct was built around the history of white supremacy. Furthermore, it elucidates the way the ideology of white supremacy was sustained by the narrative of racial difference, and it connects that narrative to modern incarnations of racism.

This quote is helpful for another reason as well—a reason of particular importance for Christians: it helps us see the ways in which racism is a spiritual problem and how the ongoing support of it directly defies the heart and character of God. We could view the narrative of racial difference from many theological angles, but at the top of the list is the way it denies the biblical understanding of what it means to be human.

The creation account in Genesis 1 famously opens with the words "In the beginning God created the heavens and the earth" and then goes on to chronicle God's activities throughout the first six days. It concludes with the culminating act of God's divine power—the creation of humankind:

> Then God said, "Let us make mankind in our image, in our likeness, so that they may rule over the fish in the sea and the birds in the sky, over the livestock and all the wild animals, and over all the creatures that move along the ground."

> So God created mankind in his own image,
>   in the image of God he created them;
>   male and female he created them. (Genesis 1:26-27)

This passage reveals the splendor of the doctrine of the *imago Dei*, which holds that all human beings are created in the image and likeness of God. In Scripture, the *imago Dei* is applied exclusively to humans, highlighting the unique qualities with which we have been divinely endowed. Genesis 1 therefore is the first signpost of the "good news" of the gospel in the biblical account; it affirms that human beings are good, are of infinite value, and are a reflection of the character of the triune God.

The introduction of the *imago Dei* in Genesis 1 was a declaration of multiple truths, but chief among them was the establishment of a standard for human value and worth that would be carried throughout Scripture. The doctrine explicitly reaffirms human value at numerous points throughout the Bible (such as Genesis 5:1-3; 9:6; Psalm 8;

1 Corinthians 11:7; Colossians 3:9-10; James 3:9). Along the way are places where a writer simply stops and dwells on the magnificence of the doctrine.

King David, for example, regularly referred to the *imago Dei* in his poems, psalms, and songs. One of my favorites was when he asked,

> What is mankind that you are mindful of them,
> human beings that you care for them?
> You have made them a little lower than the angels
> and crowned them with glory and honor. (Psalm 8:4-5)

He took the implications of the *imago Dei* so far that it can make us uncomfortable. Isn't it incredible that we are a little lower than the angels and crowned with glory and honor?

Passages like this played a role in shaping the works of giants like C. S. Lewis, who was one of the heavyweight thinkers of the twentieth century. When meditating on the *imago Dei*, he came up with the concept of "the weight of glory," a phrase he used to name both a sermon and a book. He believed that because each person reflects the very glory of God, we should value humanity accordingly. He wrote, "It is a serious thing to live in a society of possible gods and goddesses. . . . There are no ordinary people. You have never talked to a mere mortal."[14]

It's important to wrap our minds around the doctrine of the *imago Dei* because it's a theological foundation we must stand on as we learn to critique and condemn the social construct of race in America and our historical reliance on white supremacy. Stated simply, the *imago Dei* declares that all human beings are valuable and of infinite worth. God is the one that makes this declaration, and no human being is allowed to challenge it. To do so is to play God. Yet when we created the American construct of race, that's exactly what we did. We undercut the *imago Dei* by establishing the narrative of racial difference.

The fact that we *recognize* racial difference is not the issue. The theological danger comes with a system of race that *assigns value* based on the differences. Assigning value to human beings is in direct contradiction to the heart of God, and it is a sin of the highest order.

Now let's name what the narrative of racial difference reveals to each of us.

First, it helps us to identify the *sin* behind racism. When we see an individual act of racism, most of us are comfortable labeling it a sin. But if our vision is limited to individual acts of racism, we are unable to understand both the world and ourselves. The original narrative of racial difference was built on a lie—the lie that human beings can be valued along a racial spectrum. The sin behind this lie touches every part of our society. Seeing the presence of the narrative of racial difference positions us to join the redemptive work of Jesus Christ in a unique and powerful way.

Second, the narrative of racial difference can help us decipher the messages that have informed our understanding of cultural identity, which has formed in the midst of a heated contest between two competing ideologies: that narrative and the *imago Dei*. To live in America, especially as a Christian, is to be bombarded by diametrically opposing messages. The narrative of racial difference promotes a valuation of life measured along a racial continuum with a sliding scale, which dehumanizes both people of color and people who are white. The doctrine of the *imago Dei* insists on recognizing every human being as an image bearer of God and therefore as valuable and worthy. To live from our identity in Christ, we must confront the ways the narrative has informed both our sense of self and our views of other people.

The Narrative's Infection of Social Systems

When left unchallenged, the narrative of racial difference inflicts catastrophic damage on every level of society, starting at an individual level moving into communities of people before infecting the roots of our social systems. We need a transformed vision that recognizes the narrative at each level, but we especially need to learn to see the impact of the narrative on our social systems.

A social system is made up of the elements that work together in towns and cities, such as schools, police departments, businesses and manufacturing, hospitals, grocery stores, housing, and other entities. Though these entities provide services or play certain roles, they also form what is often called a social system. Each element within a social system is supposed to serve people of all backgrounds equally, regardless of race or any other social marker. But the narrative of racial difference prevents that because it is built around a calculation of human value based on race, which reproduces inequalities.

Let's look at education to see how the narrative poisons a social system. American education is meant to provide a standard education so all can participate in and contribute to the economy. However, statistics reveal an overwhelming discrepancy between the education provided for white students and that provided for students of color. Why is this social system working for some and failing others? The primary culprit is the narrative of racial difference.

Consider a specific example that shows the social effects of the narrative. Stephanie is an African American, an accomplished medical doctor, and a respected leader in our church. She makes most things she does look easy. Those who don't know her story may assume that her life path skirted the landmines of racism. But that's far from the truth.

Stephanie shared her story at church one Sunday, beginning by describing her parents and how their experiences of racial discrimination led them to raise her and her brother in an affluent white suburb in metro Chicago. She shared what it was like to grow up black in an all-white community and the confusion that created in her cultural identity journey.

But Stephanie focused on what she called the most pivotal year of her life: second grade. That's when her school began testing students individually for gifting in reading and math. Those who scored high were elevated to a gifted track. Stephanie was one of the top students in the class, and she was excited to see how she would perform on the tests. She watched as the teacher called in student after student for testing but not her. Even at her young age she already felt that the teacher treated her differently than the white students. That day, the difference felt very real.

That evening at the dinner table, Stephanie's mom asked how her day had gone, as she did each evening. Stephanie told her about all the activities of the day and then started telling her about the testing. Her mother asked questions, and it became clear to her that Stephanie had been overlooked. Though she was furious, she kept herself composed in front of her second grader. She knew exactly what she needed to do.

The next morning Stephanie's mother stormed into the school and asked the gifted program instructor why they had failed to include Stephanie in the testing. The instructor mumbled a confusing explanation, then looked through her records and said that she had accidentally overlooked Stephanie, blaming it on an administrative error. Stephanie took the tests that day and received top scores in both reading and math. She was placed into the gifted program and never looked back.

Stephanie now sees this was pivotal in her development, because it set an academic trajectory for the rest of her life. If her mother hadn't intervened, Stephanie wouldn't have been in advanced classes in elementary school, so she wouldn't have been on the college preparatory track in high school. And if she hadn't been on the college preparatory track, she wouldn't have been accepted into med school. And if she hadn't gone to med school, she wouldn't be the doctor she is today, serving marginalized populations that often get less-than-thorough medical care.

This story is a clear example of how the narrative of racial difference can infect a social system. In it, we don't see a cruel, racist group of people maliciously targeting students of color. In fact, I'd bet that if someone had asked the administrators and teachers in Stephanie's school, "Do you consider yourself to be a racist in any way?" every one would have said no emphatically. And if someone had asked them, "Do you think you see or treat students of color differently than white students?" I'd bet every response would be no. What does this story reveal? In a high-performing, diversity-minded school, a black second grader was treated differently than her white peers.

Is it possible there was a genuine administrative error? Sure. However, it's likely that the narrative of racial difference was at work, largely undetected. In Stephanie's case, the narrative led the teacher to assign a lower intellectual capacity to a black student than to the white students.

This illustration is just the tip of the iceberg. We need to examine other critical systems required for support and survival—employment, housing, policing, health and nutrition, and more—for the effect of the narrative. It has poisoned the roots of many of these systems and continues to reproduce disparities in the outcomes for white people and for people of color. As we become more in tune with our own cultural identity, we can join forces with other seekers of justice, and we can name and dismantle the inequitable systems that perpetuate disparities.

Seeing the Kingdom

The kingdom of God is one reality; the kingdom of this world is another altogether. It's critical that we not only differentiate between the two but also learn to see why they are so different.

The narrative of the kingdom of God is informed by the *imago Dei*—that is, every human is created in the image of God. On the other hand, a narrative informed by racial difference undergirds the kingdom of this world; it recognizes differences in God's creation and then uses those differences as a basis for measuring human worth. Because those kingdoms are diametrically opposed, we are caught in a cosmic war for the soul of humanity.

Cultural identity begins with recognizing that this war has been waged for millennia, and it has impacted us in innumerable ways. We need to ask—and even beg—Jesus to help us to see our King and the kingdom of God in ways that take us far beyond our current vision. We need to seek our identity in Christ and to search bravely for ways in which our understanding of identity has been infiltrated by the narrative of racial difference. We then need to seek to participate in Jesus' redemptive work in society as he reconciles all things to himself. To do so, we must first encounter the kingdom of this world and learn to see the ways that kingdom reigns as a principality and power of darkness (Ephesians 6:10-20).

5

Denial

I was nineteen years old and was about to meet the father of a woman I had just begun dating. While that is a daunting task for prospective boyfriends everywhere, my fear factor skyrocketed when I discovered that he worked for the local police department. Who in their right mind wants to date the daughter of a cop? Every joke I'd ever heard about a dad introducing himself to the boyfriend while holding a shotgun suddenly seemed way too real. As such, I wanted to do everything in my power to make a good impression, so I made a significant effort to get to know him. This led to one of my most vivid encounters with racism.

This officer often shared accounts of his daily exploits, and his stories tended to be pedestrian. But on this particular occasion, he shared an account that shocked me on every level. He and his partner were patrolling the neighborhood and saw a carful of African Americans driving around the neighborhood. These young men were doing nothing wrong or illegal—an admission that rolled off his lips with ease—yet he felt justified in stopping them based on nothing but their appearance. After pulling them over, each of the four men was subjected to a full-body frisk. They were required to keep their hands on the car as the officers then searched the car. Finally, one of the young men hit his breaking point. He was humiliated and angry, and he began shouting at the officers that they had no legal basis for treating him and his friends that way.

At that point, the officer took a short detour from his storytelling and began to lecture us on how young people today don't have any respect for authority. He told us that when parents fail to instill discipline in children, it's the responsibility of others to step in. I was trying hard to follow his logic, but he returned to the story at hand. In graphic detail, he went on to tell us about the beating he and his partner gave the young man who had complained—because they viewed him as disrespectful. The story was already horrible, but it managed to get even worse as he accentuated the fact that the beating happened in front of the young man's friends. It was very important to the officer that they got the point of the lesson, and he seemed to relish the fact that he got to be the teacher.

As he shared this account, all I could do was stand there in frozen silence. I was stunned not only by the immorality of his actions but also by the confidence he had in admitting to something that was so obviously illegal. I was also aware that this was the kind of story I wouldn't believe if it were delivered secondhand. If anyone else had told me, I would have been convinced they were exaggerating to make a political point. But there I was, listening to the firsthand account of one who had executed a miscarriage of justice. This was my first adult encounter with unveiled racism, and I knew it required a response.

It may seem obvious what my response *should* have been. I should have no longer minimized the reality of racial discrimination. I should have realized that the scales of justice don't weigh equally for every person. It should have been the moment when my cultural identity journey began in earnest and where I never turned back.

But it wasn't.

Instead I went on an active search for a way to cope with the tidal wave of emotions aroused by that too-close-for-comfort encounter with racism, and I exercised my privilege. I chose to walk away.

A House of Sand

Encounters like this are typically necessary for the white awakening process. And yet such an experience alone is rarely enough. A reckoning must happen with the deeper realities that we have been exposed to, and such a reckoning requires that we overcome the overwhelming temptation to move into the second stage: denial.

Why is denial a predictable stage in the cultural identity journey? This is a notoriously difficult question to answer because denial is slippery. Once it's spotted, it begins to disintegrate, and it struggles to remain undetected at all costs. (This is why we need to name it!) So, in an attempt to pin denial down, let's use my story as a test case. How could I have such a close contact with overt racism and still find a way to deny its existence?

The first answer is the way the encounter shook the whole foundation of my worldview. It was shocking for me to hear a police officer openly brag about profiling a car full of young, African American men. It was even more unsettling to hear him boast about provoking them to the point that he felt justified in assaulting one of them in order to teach a lesson in respect for authority.

As I stumbled away from that conversation, I felt shaken to the bone. Up to that point, it would have never occurred to me that a US citizen of any background would have a reason to fear the police. I remembered being taught as a child to see the increased presence of police as a strictly positive contribution to the neighborhood. I also remembered the deference with which adults in my neighborhood spoke of the importance of the men and women who took the oath and badge to protect and serve the community.

But for the first time, I had seen this authority abused. Instead of protecting and serving the entire community, an officer had targeted and essentially terrorized the black residents of this neighborhood. I wasn't presuming that the actions of this officer were representative of others. Yet since I'd seen this encounter up close, it unleashed a series of unwanted questions: *If there is one police officer targeting African Americans, are there others? What does that say about the racial views of the police department as a whole? Is it possible that many of them are good people but deeply affected by racism nonetheless? And if I'm going to make a mental allowance for the policing system, what about society as a whole? Is the vision I've clung to about our country true? Are we indeed a nation created to treat all people as equally valuable? Or have we been stained by a racist ideology that treats some of our population as second-class citizens?*

Once the floodgate opened, I struggled to stop the tide. It didn't take me long for the questions to become personal; I began to wonder if my own family structure was as race-neutral as I presumed. I had been raised with a colorblind ideology that intentionally de-emphasized racial differences in the hopes that we see all people as the same. This seemed fine in my growing-up years, but now I was wondering if that approach was flawed. I wondered, *If society treats people of color differently than it treats white people, is my colorblindness just an excuse to happily depart into la-la land? Is it possible that my grandparents, whom I adore, are part of this larger racial problem? Is it possible that my parents are part of it? And what about me? Am I part of the problem? Are we all good people that are just ignorant of race? Or worse, are we closet racists who are unwilling to acknowledge the problems out there—as well as inside of our own hearts and souls?*

In the game Jenga, each player takes a turn removing a block from a carefully stacked bunch of blocks. The goal is to avoid knocking the whole thing over by removing blocks very carefully. So you don't pull blocks from the base level because if you mess with the foundation, the whole thing could easily come toppling down. That is an imperfect but real metaphor for what my life felt like after that encounter with racism. An unending series of questions about race in America was shaking the base-level blocks of how I viewed reality. The more I considered them, the more I felt my foundation shaking. I feared that staying there too long would cause my whole worldview to come crashing down.

When I look back now, I see that this is exactly what was supposed to happen. A faulty foundation may stay propped up for a while, but it isn't worth keeping in the long run. It doesn't matter how high you build; it's still going to crash at some point. It occurred to me later that this must have been what Jesus was referring to when he said,

> Therefore everyone who hears these words of mine and puts them into practice is like a wise man who built his house on the rock. The rain came down, the streams rose, and the winds blew and beat against that house; yet it did not fall, because it had its foundation on the rock. But everyone who hears these words of mine and does not put them into practice is like a foolish man who built his house on sand. The rain came down, the streams rose, and the winds blew and beat against that house, and it fell with a great crash. (Matthew 7:24-27)

Jesus concluded the Sermon on the Mount with this image, and it summarizes the results of denial. Encounters with racism serve as the rain/water/wind storm in the lives of those of us in the dominant culture. The storm shakes us to the core and reveals what foundation is built on the rock and what foundation is built on the sand. The revelation of where our foundation lies can be terrifying, but it also can be liberating.

It's of ultimate importance that our view of reality is built on the rock and not the sand. And if we can learn to interpret the nature of these storms as a gift from Jesus, we're halfway home to defeating denial.

White Trauma

Though an individual choice to pursue wisdom and rebuff foolishness is important, we must recognize the depth of denial that grips our nation as a whole. It doesn't seem to matter how much exposure white

America has to racial injustice or how many encounters we have with systemic inequality, we can't seem to snap out of our collective slumber and admit the faults in our foundations.

I've heard Mark Charles, a theologian, speaker, and writer of Navajo heritage lecture on national denial on multiple occasions, and I credit him as the primary influence on my understanding of this subject (and many others). A sermon he gave to my own congregation sparked my appreciation of the challenges of attempting to foster a national awakening. As he specifically addressed the communities of color within River City Community Church, he first sympathized with the ongoing oppression that many of them needed to overcome. Then he moved on to suggest how they could better understand the collective denial of white America. He wrapped it around a pair of words that make a lot of conceptual sense: *white trauma.*

Charles said that reconciliation conversations tend to focus on the historical trauma that communities of color have faced, and he affirmed that this must continue to be the case. The problem, he suggested, is that the conversation around trauma stops with them. But what about the white community? While the traumas experienced by victims and by oppressors are qualitatively different on every level and can therefore never be compared, it's impossible to be complicit with centuries of traumatizing oppression without becoming traumatized oneself.

This was a groundbreaking idea for me. While I had grown to recognize the ways our racial history has traumatized communities of color, I had never considered the ways white America had also been traumatized by this same history. I had a new appreciation for why denial is such an accessible temptation for every white person: it's easy to turn a blind eye toward history at an individual level when our nation still does so at a corporate level.

When we consider some of the ways we treat history as a nation, we see the fallout from white trauma. Take Columbus Day, for example, a legal holiday recognized on the second Monday of every

October. Search it online or in almost any history book, and you're most likely to find this description: it's a holiday that commemorates the discovery of the New World by Christopher Columbus in 1492.

Discovery? Really? Can any thinking person say with a straight face that what Columbus did when he got to America was "discover"? How can one discover a nation that's already inhabited by millions? Charles highlights how ludicrous this claim is by asking his listeners to consider leaving out their wallet, phone, or iPad so they can experience what it's like to have their property "discovered."

Yet we've made the <u>conscious decision</u> to tell the history of our nation as one that was discovered by Columbus and other explorers.[1] Some questions beg to be asked: How have we convinced ourselves to embrace something that sounds more like a fairy tale than a factual account of history? How do otherwise logical people voluntarily look past the documented facts and pass on a false narrative? There is only one explanation that makes sense: We are traumatized, and we are therefore in denial. Acknowledging that all our land was stolen from Native people feels like too great a burden, so we create an alternative reality that allows us to disengage emotionally from the truth.

Another major historical reality that has shaped the fabric of the United States is the seventy-plus years of black lynchings. The Equal Justice Initiative, an organization started by Bryan Stevenson, published an important report on this topic, titled "Lynching in America: Confronting the Legacy of Racial Terror,"[2] which tells a real-life horror story that lives outside the scope of white Americans. The report documents 3,959 lynchings of black people in twelve Southern states between the end of Reconstruction in 1877 and 1950. Think about that. Close to four thousand human beings were publicly murdered for acts as simple as having a conversation with a white female.

Why do we not talk about lynchings more? In the United States, every year we honor the 2,996 people killed in the terrorist attacks on the World Trade Center, as we rightly should. But have you ever heard of an honor ceremony to acknowledge the 3,959 lives lost to lynching? And if I were going to pry, as I often do within my friendship circles, I would ask how much familiarity you have with the history of lynching. I point a finger at myself first, because I was ignorant of this history. I'm ashamed to admit that until my late twenties, I had no reference point for the word *lynching* except for people using the word as slang. I certainly had no in-depth knowledge of the history of lynching, nor could I comprehend how the terror of that period left aftershocks in the black community that have been felt for decades.

Some uncomfortable questions need to be asked. Why do we reverently remember the casualties of those attacked by terrorists from outside our country (again, as we should) but turn a blind eye to the black lives lost in acts of terror at the hands of those within our own country? Why, in an Internet search on "terrorist attacks in American history," does lynching not even appear? Why is it that most culture history books pay scant attention to lynchings?

The most plausible answer is white trauma. At a corporate level, it's traumatic that a country that aspires to be a place of equality for all people did this to its own citizens. And the risk of trauma is high at a personal level. Once we open up this history, who knows what else we'll find? I think of a white friend who came from a long line of preachers and the anxiety he felt about exploring his lineage. He knew his grandfather pastored during the height of the KKK, and he was quite apprehensive about what he might discover if he began to poke around. Versions of this same anxiety live within many of us. We want to believe our grandparents and great grandparents were noble people who were on the right side of history. But something inside of us also knows that the true story could be very different. These are traumatic possibilities, and denial always looms as a tempting option for avoiding the truth.

One last example: in my early twenties, I became close to a man of Japanese American heritage, and through our friendship I learned about the historical significance of internment camps. Did you know that two months after the bombing of Pearl Harbor, President Franklin D. Roosevelt signed an executive order that all Japanese Americans had to evacuate the West Coast? (Contrast this with the fact that no internment of German Americans occurred, despite being at war with Germany at the time.) This resulted in the forced incarceration of nearly 120,000 people, the majority of whom were US citizens, into ten internment camps across the country.

I was shocked to discover this. I then learned that in 1988 President Ronald Reagan signed into law the Civil Liberties Act, a piece of legislation that admitted to government actions being a result of "race prejudice, war hysteria, and a failure of political leadership." As a result of this admission, each camp survivor was rewarded with reparations of $20,000 each. As I learned about this recent history, I found myself again wondering how I had learned about World War II in school yet had never heard of internment camps, national admissions to racism, or the corresponding reparations. How could something this major have happened within the century and go unmentioned in a history class? By now you know my answer: white trauma is the most plausible explanation.

Lifting Up the Truth

I have already used Nicodemus as an archetype for the awakening journey, and his story once again provides a template for transformation. The conversation between Jesus and Nicodemus began with the importance of learning to "see" the kingdom through spiritual rebirth and then culminated with what is arguably the most famous verse in the Bible, John 3:16: "For God so loved the world that he gave his one and only Son, that whoever believes in him shall not perish but have eternal life." By finishing the conversation there, Jesus pronounced to Nicodemus (and to us) that the ultimate expression of "seeing" the kingdom of God is to see Jesus himself. To see the kingdom is to see Jesus as the beloved Son. To see the kingdom is to Jesus as the ultimate incarnational expression of God's love. To see the kingdom is to see that life is found through Jesus Christ alone.

The unique way that Jesus proclaimed the gospel in John 3 is incredible enough, but he also provided a significant biblical resource for addressing national trauma. Just before he talked about how God sent his beloved Son into the world, Jesus said this: "As Moses lifted up the serpent in the wilderness, so the Son of Man must be lifted up, that everyone who believes may have eternal life in him" (vv. 14-15).

When Jesus alluded to Moses lifting up the serpent, he was drawing from a story in Numbers 21 that describes one of the more traumatic experiences of the Israelite community in Old Testament times. Carlos Ruiz, a pastor at River City for close to ten years and a therapist, wrote this in a chapter on trauma in *Intercultural Ministry: Hope for a Changing World*:

> A biblical story that has been helpful to me as a paradigm of healing is found in Numbers 21. When the Israelites were in the wilderness and then, after sinning against God, serpents came out and bit them, leaving many Israelites dead in the desert. They must have experienced a traumatic terror as they saw friends and family being attacked and dying by the frightening serpents. After they repented of their sin and asked for help to Moses, it would have made sense for God to remove the serpents right away in order to heal them. However, God did not do that. On the contrary, God asked Moses to build an icon of the very creature that was causing them to die, a serpent of bronze. Whenever they would look at the serpent of bronze, they would be healed and live. In this story God tells Moses that they need to look at the figure of the snake of bronze so that people could be healed and live . . . an odd way of being saved. It is odd and scary because they realized that if they looked at the traumatic icon, instead of running away from it they would live.

When I think about this story, I cannot help but think that similar situations are occurring in our communities today. There is in all of us, especially in our environments where we want to pursue and experience reconciliation, a big desire to move on and not look at the snakes that have come out to bite and kill for generations. We are afraid, we are helpless, and we are ashamed of the little "progress" we have made to the point that we want to push harder or completely disengage. The story of the serpent of bronze doesn't let us do either of those options. On the contrary it tells us that we need to look at our own serpent of bronze if we want to embrace healing and live. The very trauma we suffer and want to escape from is the very trauma we need to look at.[3]

This would have been an extremely traumatic experience for the nation of Israel, and it would have been understandable if they had attempted everything in their power to put distance between themselves and this distressing memory. It must have been tempting to forget it happened, to bury it, or at least to try to minimize it. And if they couldn't outright forget it, it would have been tempting to at least revise the history to make it more palatable. But God refused to give them the option of national denial. Instead God insisted that they look *directly* at the trauma if they wanted to embrace healing and life.

Why does God ask traumatized people to look at the trauma they initiated through their sin and rebellion? For the same reason God asks us to: it is the truth, and we are free only when we lift up the truth.

This is why denial is such a dangerous coping mechanism. While it may lull us into a feeling of temporary comfort, it means living in a lie. I want to be cautious about overstating this, but it would seem that the words of Jesus suggest the possibility that denial (or any other form of lying) is not only dangerous but also demonic. One of Jesus' most terrifying statements came in response to a group of Pharisees who refused to acknowledge truth: "Why is my language not clear to you? Because you are unable to hear what I say. You belong to your father, the devil, and you want to carry out your father's desires. He was a murderer from the beginning, not holding to the truth, for there is no truth in him. When he lies, he speaks his native language, for he is a liar and the father of lies" (John 8:43-44).

Jesus said that the native language of the devil is lies, and he graphically warned against any alignment with the one who not only lies but whose very identity is rooted in those lies. While denial often presents itself as a lesser version of lying, we must be vigilant to avoid being deceived about its treacherous nature.

If the native language of the evil one is lies, we can safely say the native language of God is truth. Upon our conversion, the Spirit of God immediately begins to guide us into all truth (John 16:13). This truth is what connects us to the very person of Jesus (John 14:6) and what ultimately leads to deliverance and healing. In the same passage where Jesus condemns the deceitful nature of the evil one, he triumphantly holds up the power of truth: "Then you will know the truth, and the truth will set you free" (John 8:32).

There are powerful examples of nations that have followed this path in recent memory, and we would do well to learn from their example. In Germany, for example, the shadow of the Holocaust looms large, and it must have been tempting for Germans to fall into the trap of denial. But instead of revising the historical narrative, they have consistently and courageously lifted up the truth. If you visit Berlin, you will see many monuments marking the places where Jewish families were abducted from their homes and transported to concentration camps. Germany is searching for healing not by running from the truth but by lifting it up.

South Africa knew the only way to pursue healing after apartheid was to acknowledge that history honestly, and in 1996 the Truth and Reconciliation Commission was formed. In 1999, Rwanda formed the

National Unity and Reconciliation Commission to address the genocide their country had experienced. Canada launched a similar commission in 2008 in an effort to comprehensively acknowledge and address charges of abuse to First Nations children at residential schools. All of these serve as models for beginning to chart a national course for lifting up the truth.

A Common Memory

When addressing the reality of white trauma, Mark Charles regularly quotes Georges Erasmus, an Aboriginal advocate, political leader, and well-respected spokesperson for indigenous peoples in Canada. Erasmus says, "Where common memory is lacking, where people do not share in the same past, there can be no real community. Where community is to be formed, common memory must be created."

As Charles points out, this quote gets to the heart of both nations' problems with race: our citizens do not share a common memory. People of white European ancestry remember a history of discovery, open lands, manifest destiny, endless opportunity, and American exceptionalism. Yet communities of color, especially those with African and indigenous roots, remember a history of stolen lands, broken treaties, slavery, boarding schools, segregation, cultural genocide, internment camps, and mass incarceration.[4]

This is the choice that lies before us both as a nation and as individuals: Will we continue to live in denial and allow our home to be built on the weak foundation of myths and half-truths? Or will we have the courage to live up to the truth and allow God's holy fire to burn down the old and erect a new home that can hold us all?

These are the salient questions of the denial stage. With an encounter comes the beginning of an awakening, but awakening always requires that we choose a path. Denial or truth? Sand or rock? Fear or courage?

Let us boldly choose to follow the One who is Truth.

6

Disorientation

One of my favorite miracles happens in Mark 8. While Jesus was walking through Bethsaida, some people brought a blind man to him and begged for a supernatural intervention. Jesus agreed, though what he did next is a bit odd. He initiated the healing process by spitting into his hands. I can't help but wonder what the blind man thought as he listened to the famous and powerful rabbi form a spitball.

Once Jesus had accumulated the appropriate amount of divine saliva, he wiped it across the eyes of the blind man. He then asked, "Do you see anything?" (v. 23).

The blind man was uncertain if healing had taken place. There was noticeable progress, as now he was able to see shadows, but his inability to process images showed that the healing was far from complete. The blind man responded to Jesus by simply saying, "I see people; they look like trees walking around" (v. 24).

This miracle has been a parable for my own white-awake journey. Like the blind man, I've experienced the healing touch of Jesus. I've had transformational moments when I went from utter blindness to being able to see the light.

But as beautiful as these have been, I've often found myself disoriented and saying a version of the same thing as the blind man. I still mistake people for trees, reminding me that the healing is not yet complete. In the words of the influential twentieth-century evangelic David Martyn-Lloyd Jones, I am "stuck between touches."

Drew Hart, the African American author of *The Trouble I've Seen*, tells a story that I've come back to often when thinking about the disorientation that often accompanies the cultural identity journey. Hart recounts an experience at a conference focused on faith and justice. While he looked forward to the conference as a whole, he most eagerly anticipated the invitation-only small-group conversation for those involved with addressing racial justice. The topic was the incompatibility of white supremacy and faith in Jesus Christ, and as an activist and theologian, this was a conversation he longed to have.

Hart went to the meeting wondering what the transparency level would be and left pleasantly surprised by the combination of candor and grace. There was honest conversation around the difficulty of working against the ideology of white supremacy but also a clear sense that faith was motivating each of the individuals to move toward a kingdom ideology of human equality, even when the cost seemed high.

Hart walked away from the meeting feeling renewed and invigorated. As he prepared to return to the general session, a white woman from the group tapped him on the shoulder and asked if they could debrief together for a few minutes. He wasn't sure what she needed or why she chose him, but he agreed.

They found a seat out of the path of traffic, and she told him she perceived him to be a safe person to process the disorientation with and then said her emotions had felt charged by the meeting. She took a few stabs at attempting to name what was bothering her and finally decided to put it in the form of a question: "What did you think about how people were saying white people can't be Christian?"

This question surprised him, because nothing even close to that had been said. He thought the discussion had separated the conversation about white superiority from the conversation about individuals who are white, and he hadn't heard anything about white people being unable to be Christians. So he assumed she had misheard what was being said and then took the time to contrast the *system* of whiteness with the inherent human value of white *individuals* affected by that system. He reassured her that the conversation was attacking neither the humanity of white people nor their Christianity.

Though his response was cogent and clear, it did little to calm her. In fact, with each additional clarification, her sadness grew. Finally, uncontrollable tears began to flow down her face.

Hart paused, contemplating what he would do next. "White tears" like those were nothing new for him. Because the contents unearthed during explorations of race can be so overwhelming—and at times even threatening—to white people who are new to the conversation, significant feelings often need to be accommodated for those in the early stages of the journey. Seasoned crosscultural facilitators know this.

Yet this woman hadn't presented herself as new to the conversation of race. She understood that it was an invitation-only small group and that it had been billed as an opportunity to have candid conversations about racial justice. The fact that she chose to attend meant that she viewed herself as more than a beginner. As such, Hart decided to engage her at a more advanced level and to treat her like an adult.

Instead of jumping to reassure her at the point of her emotional fragility, as he sometimes did with people new to the cultural identity journey, Hart urged her to stay with her feelings for as long as she could. He encouraged her to embrace and analyze the feelings of disorientation and then asked her to consider some reflection questions. She was game for doing her best, so he proposed some questions like these:

- Why did a conversation around American history provoke such a deep emotional response?

- Why did you have a different recollection of the conversation than I did? How did I see it as candid but gracious, but you saw it as hostile to white people?

◆ Why did you come to the invitation-only meeting on race? What did you hope to gain from the conversation?

Hart was gracious but firm as he led her through this process, and then he brought her to the disorientation, which is being explored in this chapter. He asked her to consider this: Was it possible that her conflicting emotions from this conversation were a sign that she was drawing too much of her sense of worth from being white? Was it possible that in the development of her identity and sense of self-worth cultural cues about whiteness were playing a more formative role than the words of God were?

From Blindness to Sight

This story illustrates the disorientation that consistently accompanies moving from blindness to sight. Like the man who had been partially healed of blindness in Mark 8, the woman in this story found herself "stuck between touches." On one hand, she had already embarked on an important journey of transformation—she would have never been drawn to an intimate conversation on racial justice if she hadn't. On the other hand, she wasn't nearly as far along as she had hoped, a discovery that came the hard way at the small-group meeting.

I relate to the story of this woman, as disorientation has accompanied my cultural identity process at every stage. My journey began in the Willow Creek days with a series of light bulbs on race going off. But as I pondered how to move forward, I could find nothing inside other than a vague disorientation. My journey continued with the launch of Metro 212 and the dream of building a culturally diverse ministry. But when I was unable to reach beyond my white community, I became overwhelmed by disorientation. Then I met with the four pastors, desperate for answers to my growing list of questions. Instead of finding clarity, I came away feeling even more disoriented. That pattern has remained true at River City as well. Each era of growth for our community has been beautiful but has also overlapped with confusion about what to do next.

Disorientation is an unavoidable stage if you embark seriously on a cultural identity journey, so it's not worth investing energy in a futile attempt to avoid those feelings. It's more helpful to understand *why* we feel disoriented and to learn to push forward even as we feel uncertain of our footing.

As you follow the transformational path from blindness to sight, a variety of factors may lead to disorientation. Each is important to understand, and each needs to be conquered if you are to keep moving forward. Here are the four most significant contributors to the disorientation stage:

- lack of exposure
- low stamina
- limited theological understanding
- crisis of identity

Lack of Exposure

In chapter one, I shared about the day I discovered my world was white. It took me so long to discover that because I would have argued the opposite if given the chance. In my elementary school years, I lived in an all-white neighborhood bordered by an all-black neighborhood. So I had at least peripheral contact with kids of color in my age range. Then, due to the way our neighborhood was zoned, I spent my junior high years in a mostly black school. While that was the last point in my adolescent life when I was heavily immersed in a nonwhite culture, it set the stage for me to develop and maintain crosscultural relationships through my teenage, college, and post-college years. These relationships made it easy to dismiss the possibility that I had a white perspective on life.

That's why I initially fought back when my first mentor on race proposed that my world was cut off from the voices of people of color. I was quick to point to the demographics of my childhood neighborhood, my junior high experience, and most importantly, my small but real roster of friends who weren't white. Not until he gave me the self-reflection exercise did my vantage point finally change. Again, rather than allowing me to gauge my cultural identity using nominal relationships with people outside my life circles, he challenged me to assess the four voices that were shaping me: friends, mentors, preachers/teachers/theologians, and authors of the books I was reading.

Well, as it turns out, I'm not the only one living in an all-white world. In his standup routine on race, entitled "Kill the Messenger," Chris Rock highlights the segregated nature of white America, saying, "All my black friends have a bunch of white friends. And all my white friends have *one* black friend." Data shows that across the country, this is more than just a funny joke—it's our reality.

For example, an article on friendships across racial lines gives an overview of the results of a Public Religion Research Institute study of racial segregation. The study measured the percentages of a typical white person's friendship network. In a one-hundred-friend scenario, the data showed that the average white person has ninety-one white friends; one each of black, Latino, Asian, mixed race, and other races; and three friends of unknown races. So, when comparing the social network of black Americans to white Americans specifically, the results showed that white Americans had an astonishing ninety-one times as many white friends as black friends.[1]

Dr. Robin DiAngelo, a professor of multicultural education at Westfield State University, is widely considered to be an authority in this area. She lectures nationally on the nature of white culture and codesigned, developed, and delivered the City of Seattle Race and Social Justice Initiative Anti-Racism training. She wrote a widely referred to piece entitled "White Fragility," pointing to social segregation as the number-one reason for the term. In it, she wrote,

> The first factor leading to White Fragility is the segregated lives which most white people live. . . . Even if whites live in physical proximity to people of color (and this would be exceptional outside of an urban or temporarily mixed class neighborhood), segregation occurs on multiple levels, including representational and informational. Because whites live primarily segregated lives in a white-dominated society, they receive little or no authentic information about racism and are thus unprepared to think about it critically or with complexity. Growing up in segregated environments (schools, workplaces, neighborhoods, media images and historical perspectives), white interests and perspectives are almost always central. An inability to see or consider significance in the perspectives of people of color results.[2]

So the first reason white people experience disorientation is a lack of exposure to authentic interaction and engagement with race. For the most part, white Americans are raised in and continue to live in segregated settings. Even when a person has contact with people of color, rarely do relationships deepen to the point of exchanging meaningful ideas about the system of race. Therefore, it's important to acknowledge our "representational and informational" segregation.[3] In chapter ten, I propose a number of different ideas for reversing this trend and actively encourage finding new ways to become proximate to and to learn from those whom we are segregated from.

Low Stamina

I was recently invited to join an intentionally multiethnic small group of pastors from the city of Chicago to meet once a month over a year. The white pastor who launched the group had experienced the beginnings of a racial awakening, and he was becoming restless over the state of racial affairs in the city. This is understandable, as the larger church in Chicago is just as segregated as its individual neighborhoods, and his conviction was growing that clergy should lead the way in demonstrating unity across racial lines.

I agree with this sentiment wholeheartedly, but I've become cynical about attempts like his. I've participated in a number of similar endeavors over the years, and they rarely have staying power. A big reason why, unfortunately, is that the white pastors in the group run out of steam quickly. When their investment decreases, the clergy of color get discouraged, and the group disbands. That being said, I appreciated the enthusiasm of this pastor. He had recruited a number of pastors of color into the group, so I willingly joined.

The convening pastor brought a printed agenda to the first meeting and was excited to propose some issues that he thought this multi-ethnic group could address. The conversation started with his agenda points but quickly changed course toward issues of racial justice. The pastors of color were gravely concerned about violence, poverty, and a host of other challenges affecting the communities where they were serving, and those issues dominated the conversation.

When we gathered a second time, the convening pastor made another attempt at facilitating a conversation around his prepared agenda. But racial justice quickly became the center again, and we had another robust discussion about if and how we could partner to address the challenges facing our communities.

When the third meeting came, the convening pastor shared that he was confused about how he should participate. He confessed that he had been hoping to discuss a number of issues, particularly around church leadership and theology, but those issues were being eclipsed by the issues associated with racial justice.

One of members immediately challenged this notion and attempted to reframe the lead pastor's frustration as an opportunity for growth: "Maybe you came into this group looking to grow in one area, but God had a plan for you to grow in a different area."

The pastor replied, "Maybe—" then paused, apparently trying to decide how honest he wanted to be. He chose to be forthright (for which I was grateful) and finished his thought: "One of the challenges I feel with being a pastor in general is managing my time and my energy. I have only so much of it to give. When I get a chance to talk with other pastors about theology and church leadership, I feel energized, and it seems clear that it's a good use of my time. But if I'm honest, these issues around race make me feel drained, and I walked away from the first two discussions feeling completely tired."

His comments hung in the air for what seemed like an eternity, and finally a black pastor responded with the perfect combination of truth and love. He looked this white pastor in the eye and said, "If you think you're tired, imagine how I feel. You're talking about this once a month for two hours, and then you go back into environments where you can stop thinking about these issues. I don't ever get the opportunity to turn this conversation off. The livelihood of my family depends on these issues. The livelihood of my congregation depends on these issues. I don't have the luxury to pick and choose when I talk about this. If the Christian faith doesn't speak to these issues in my community, then that faith would be irrelevant."

Nobody was sure how the white pastor would respond, but to his credit, he was gracious and receptive. After pondering the words of this black pastor, he admitted that he'd never considered how privileged he was to be able to come in and out of conversations without any real cost. He also acknowledged that "tired" for him couldn't compare to the fatigue of being a person of color talking about issues of race on a daily and even hourly basis. His confession opened a door to a new level of growth in his cultural identity process and positioned him to go to new depths in his journey from blindness to sight.

His story also is a helpful illustration of how stamina plays a major role in the disorientation stage for white people. One of the manifestations of privilege that comes with white skin in America is being sheltered from having to engage with "race-based stress," a term DiAngelo uses when describing white fragility. "White people in North America live in a social environment that protects and insulates them from race-based stress," she says. "This insulated environment of racial protection builds white expectations for racial comfort while at the same time lowering the ability to tolerate racial stress, leading to what I refer to as White Fragility."[4]

It's hard to dispute the fact that the experience of growing up white in America is different from growing up as a person of color. We've already explored the racial stress that comes with the development of cultural identity for people of color in America; they are consistently measured against the white norm and have to find a way to reconcile their own worth in light of the mixed messages culture sends to them. This stress is both unavoidable and significant in cost. I wouldn't go so far as to call it a silver lining, but one result of this reality is that it builds stamina in those who are consistently exposed to it—a stamina that white people do not possess.

Therefore, when white people decide to engage in meaningful cultural identity processes, we're choosing to say no to the privilege of avoiding race-based stress, and that direction should always be encouraged. With that being said, we also need to realize that the privilege of mobility does not disappear with this positive movement; we will continue to be able to choose whether or not to stay engaged once we're exposed to race-based stress. In DiAngelo's words, when our "racial comfort" is challenged and our low stamina for engaging racial stress is revealed, we need to find a way to stay in the game.

DiAngelo often tells her audience that white people tend to confuse comfort with safety, and that can be a helpful idea when navigating the disoriented stage. Because our stamina is low and tolerance for racial stress is weak, we often have conversations about racial justice being unsafe (consider the opening story from Drew Hart as an example of this). But it's rare that these situations are actually unsafe; they're uncomfortable because we aren't accustomed to that level of discourse.

So the second reason white people experience disorientation is due to having little stamina for race-based stress. To be white is to be sheltered from that type of stress. The hopeful news is that stamina is like a muscle in that it can be strengthened through training and exercise. When you engage with difficult topics, as you're doing right now, you develop a more muscular approach to staying engaged.

Limited Theological Understanding

Lecrae is a successful hip-hop artist and Grammy winner, and his rise to fame was largely based on the support of his white evangelical fan base. This same group makes up most of his one million–plus Twitter following, and many of them were grateful that in the early years of his career he rarely talked about race. But that was also the reason many of them turned on him when he posted a tweet with a photo on a Fourth of July weekend. The photo showed a group of African Americans in a field picking cotton. The caption read, "My family on July 4th 1776."[5]

The backlash to the tweet was as fast as it was furious. Thousands of white Christians protested what they perceived to be an unnecessarily provocative message, and many of them called for Lecrae to take the tweet down. Why did they have such a negative reaction to a tweet that conveyed a historically accurate fact?

Part of this reaction can be blamed on denial. Independence Day in America tends to be a particularly difficult time for both those who are aware of our history and those who are not, and emotions tend to be charged when these two groups interact. But there was another dynamic at play as well, and it had to do more with Christian theology than it did American history. This thread could be seen throughout the tens of thousands of comments, but two of the more popular responses summarize it well:

> Done supporting you bro. You make everything a race issue lately instead of a gospel issue.
>
> The race card needs to go, and Christ needs to be at the center.

The charge leveled at Lecrae was the same charge that every Christian who does justice work in the name of Christ hears at some point: He was accused of making everything a "race issue" instead of a "gospel issue."

 This is problematic in many ways, but most pressing is the way in which it bifurcates our understanding of the gospel. For reasons that go beyond what I can explore in this section, American Christianity (particularly evangelicalism) has often lost sight of a holistic understanding of the gospel. There's an emphasis on proclamation of the good news, but it tends to be theologically disconnected from demonstration of that good news. There's an emphasis on loving God as expressed in the Great Commandment, but it's theologically disconnected from loving neighbor. There's an emphasis on being reconciled to God through Christ, but it's theologically disconnected from being sent into the world by Christ as ambassadors of reconciliation (2 Corinthians 5:20).

These are sweeping statements, of course, and by speaking so broadly I risk overstating the issue. But that doesn't change my conviction that—especially for those who are white and have grown up in a theologically conservative Christian tradition—the chances are high that our theology is too limited for the work that lies ahead. Some theological giants have written entire works on this, and I explored how we can root ourselves in a more holistic theology in my previous book.[6]

Here's one example to illustrate how significant the implications are of a limited theology: Dr. Klyne Snodgrass, a New Testament scholar who is widely considered to be an expert in his field, is dismayed by the persistent theological imbalance reflected by the way we often encourage people to "invite Jesus into their hearts." This has been the dominant form of evangelistic invitation to faith in America over the past few decades, and it creates an assumption that the Christian life is primarily about asking Jesus to reside within the various dimensions of a person's inner life.

Dr. Snodgrass is quick to point out that there's nothing theologically wrong with this invitation. In his studies of the apostle Paul, he has found that there are at least five places where the language of Christ "in us" or "in me" is used. We can detect an imbalance when we look at this through a larger frame. When the apostle Paul wrote about the nature of Christian faith, he most frequently noted how we are to be "in Christ," a phrase used an astonishing 164 times. If we're told that Christ can come "in us" five times, but we are told to be "in Christ" 164 times, where should the emphasis fall in the way we talk about this? To draw out this contrast, Snodgrass says, "If Christ is only in you, then how big is Christ? Not very big, and you can tuck him away when you don't need him. But, if you and all other human beings are in Christ, as well as all of Creation, then how big is Christ?"[7]

If our view of Christianity is limited to Christ being "in me" or "in us," we will never have the theological resources to join him in works of reconciliation and justice. But if our view is expanded to see faith as fundamentally about being "in Christ," our framework changes. Our very identity is seen through the lens of being joined to Christ, and we look to participate in the kingdom work Jesus is always doing.

This is one of the ways limited theology can prevent us from fully experiencing the life Jesus Christ is inviting us into. It's just the tip of the proverbial iceberg; much more could be said about the theological resources necessary for engaging the cultural identity journey. My point in this section, however, is to emphasize the way our theological limitations contribute to the disorientation stage, so let's look at one more example to underscore the point.

When people are ready to become members at River City, they sign up for a three-week membership course. While we cover some of the specific elements of our local vision in that class, the bulk of the time is spent talking through theology. I believe that what we think about God shapes us more than anything, so the course focuses on some of the key aspects of God's character and purpose. One whole week of the class focuses on the word *reconciliation*, the linchpin of almost every letter from the apostle Paul. I believe *reconciliation* is the single best word in the Christian lexicon for communicating the full nature of our walk with God, yet few appreciate the ways this word saturates the New Testament.

At the end of each class, we leave time for participants to share their observations and questions. During one of the sessions on reconciliation, a woman began to weep, and when the tears finally began to slow down, she shared a profound observation. "I have been part of River City for a year now, and though I love the vision for reconciliation here, I often find myself feeling very disoriented by it. I grew up in church my whole life, and whenever I visit my family back home, they ask me how things are going at River City. I tell them about what we're doing, and they look at me like I'm talking in a different language. They'll slip in a comment like 'I hope they preach the gospel there too,' or 'I hope the social agenda there doesn't over-shadow what is most important to God.' I find myself thinking those same thoughts when I'm here. But now, as I study these passages that are all built around the word *reconciliation*, I realize we are preaching the gospel here. In fact, how could one preach the gospel without talking about reconciliation?"

She paused for a moment and then asked a question that's as piercing to me now as it was then: "How did I grow up in a Bible-believing church yet never once learned about the ministry of reconciliation?"

That question is a summary for what I'm hoping to convey in this section. Theology should inform the way we live each day "in Christ," yet many of us have inherited a limited foundation as our theological starting point. For a host of different reasons, there has been a split in many conservative Christian traditions between a person's personal walk with God (that is, "Christ in me") and the missional call to join the work of Christ in the world (that is, "in Christ"). This split is dangerous and results in imbalance when a follower of Jesus resides too long on one side or the other.

 If (and hopefully when) you follow Jesus into serious engagement with cultural identity, reconciliation, and other kinds of work associated with the kingdom of God, you will risk having your actions, motivations, and even maturity called into question by certain Christians. This will lead to disorientation.

Identity Crisis

At the beginning of this chapter, we learned about Drew Hart coaching a white woman through her intense feelings of disorientation. She was having trouble processing the feelings that were aroused by a candid discussion of race, so he had her reflect on a series of questions. Each of them was insightful, but there was one in particular that cut right to the bone. He sensed that she was having a crisis of identity, and he asked her if it was possible that part of the cause of the crisis was that she was still drawing a substantial amount of her self-worth from being white.

This question resonates with me because I believe it points to the greatest source of disorientation. At the heart of the awakening journey is an ongoing crisis of identity; it is an admission of an internal civil war that started long before we had the words to describe it, and it will follow us all the way to the end of the story. To be both a white Christian and a white American is to be caught between two warring factions. We may not like this, and we often struggle to acknowledge the depth of the conflict, but both of these identity sources remain at war as they vie for supremacy in our lives.

To be born white in America is to be instantly thrust into this war. Robin DiAngelo effectively demonstrates some of the ways that the ideology of white supremacy is designed to have an immediate impact on our emerging sense of identity:

> Think about it like this: from the time I opened my eyes, I have been told that as a white person, I am superior to people of color. There's never been a space in which I have not been receiving that message. From what hospital I was allowed to be born in, to how my mother was treated by the staff, to who owned the hospital, to who cleaned the rooms and took out the garbage. We are born into a racial hierarchy, and every interaction with media and culture confirms it—our sense that, at a fundamental level, we are superior. And, the thing is, it feels good. Even though it contradicts our most basic principles and values. So we know it, but we can never admit it. . . . We have set the world up to preserve that internal sense of superiority and also resist challenges to it.[8]

Becoming a Christian who is also white should mean rejecting the ideology of white superiority. Our allegiance to Jesus should enable us to recognize that this ideology is antithetical to the Bible, as is any system, ideology, or narrative that attempts to position one group of people as superior. The gospel should instead position us to draw our identity from a different source. We are told that we are created in the glorious image of God, saved through the atoning work of Christ, sealed by the Spirit of God, and delighted in by a loving Father. This is the raw material of authentic transformation.

The thrust of this book is to strengthen our ability to live from our identity in Christ while rejecting the ideology of white superiority. So, how do we manage the disorientation that comes with the internal civil war sparked by this struggle? In the same way that it would be naive for new Christians to presume that conversion comprehensively and immediately removes sin from their lives, so it is naive to assume that conversion keeps us from drawing our sense of identity from the ideology of white superiority. A good way to think of it is that conversion gives us the *ability to begin* divesting ourselves from the grips of white superiority.

The transformation of sight is often a painful process, just as all true growth is. As we move toward the brilliance of the light, we discover how much darkness was in us at each stage. This is a disorienting and confusing process, and if we don't lean into the grace of God, we are tempted to depart from the journey of transformation. Therefore, one of the most important things to remember is that, despite the disorientation that comes with a crisis of identity, it's a gift to be embraced. Each time we discover a new manifestation of white superiority that's informing our identity, we can courageously admit it, confess it, and replace it with the words of God. We remember that we have been identified by God and named as the beloved. We remember that we have been baptized into both the death and the resurrection of Christ. We remember that we are new creations, sent into God's world as ambassadors of reconciliation.

Pushing Toward the Light

In this chapter, we covered four reasons we experience disorientation and then four practices for combating those: we must move from segregation to proximity; we must strengthen ourselves and increase our stamina for tolerating racial discomfort; we must grow and deepen our theology; and we must search ruthlessly for and assess the ways white superiority informs our identity.

While there are specific nuances to each of those four, this stage lends itself to a singular summarizing application. To succinctly state how we overcome the disorientation stage, we could use the single word *resiliency.*

In the bestselling book *Resilience: Why Things Bounce Back,* Andrew Zolli (a fellow with the National Geographic Society) and Ann Marie

Healy (a playwright and journalist) define resiliency as "an ability to recover, persist or even thrive amid disruption."[9]

Disruption is a good adjective for what happens throughout the disorientation stage: It is disrupting to be exposed for a lack of knowledge or to run out of stamina. It is disrupting to lack theological resources or to discover that your identity is more compromised by white superiority than you want to admit.

The big question is, what will you do when you hit one of these disruptions? The resilient person *recovers from* disruption. The resilient person *persists through* disruption. The resilient person even learns to *thrive amid* disruption.

An experience during the early days of River City sealed this lesson for me. A group of leaders from each of the racial groups represented in our church committed to participate in a ten-week small group that explored issues of race and justice—and it was a transformative time for all of us. One of the key takeaways for white people in the group was a direct result of the admission that disorientation had set in. One of the women in the group said something like this to the people of color: "I'm honored to participate in this group, and I thank each of you profusely for the open and honest sharing. I love you and can't believe all that you have had to go through. I feel like I have to make a confession though. My head is spinning, and I feel so confused. I've never been exposed to any of this reality, and I feel like my world has been flipped upside down. I'm having trouble understanding why God would let all of this happen, what my own complicity is in it, and what this means for my life going forward. I apologize because I feel like I don't even know how to put one foot in front of the other right now."

I remember hanging my head in shame at that moment. Her words represented me as well, but I was too embarrassed to admit it (especially since I was the pastor). I expected some sort of rebuke for her honest admission and tried to position myself to take it.

But that's not what happened. Instead, one of the elders of the church said, "I appreciate you apologizing, but we don't need your apologies. What we need is your resilience. It's okay that you're feeling weak, disoriented, and unclear as what to do. What's *not* okay is that you quit because of those feelings. I need you to be resilient and to stick in the game and to walk alongside us who have no choice but to move forward."

7

Shame

At a conference focused on community development I met Jeremy, a white man actively involved in developing affordable housing in the city where he lived. When he attended my workshop on white identity, he felt a strong connection to my story. He had worked on staff at a large, white, suburban church, as I had, and he could point to a definitive racial awakening there that led him into his role. He asked if we could meet for coffee after the workshop.

When we sat down to meet, the thing that jumped out at me was Jeremy's energy and enthusiasm. It was apparent that he had a lot of passion for the work of justice, and he was excited to share about the good work he and his team were doing. It was also apparent to me that he didn't like other white people very much. I first noticed it in the negative way he described the church he had attended and worked in before his current role, but I figured that had to do with unresolved hurt from the way he transitioned out. But then he began to talk about the white residents in the city where he ministered, describing them with a great deal of disdain. This was very interesting to me, so when he finished describing all the justice initiatives he was part of, I asked him to tell me about his cultural identity journey.

Jeremy was a talker, but at that point he didn't have much to say. I tried to give him some starter questions around white identity to get him rolling, but I couldn't find an approach that helped him engage. Finally, I acknowledged the great work he was doing toward justice and asked if he had spent much time processing what it meant to be a white male doing the work he was doing.

Jeremy paused and then answered, "I have to admit I don't think about my own race much. I'm embarrassed by the history of our country, and I'm ashamed to be associated with white America. So I decided a few years ago that I would no longer identify myself as white."

Shame Versus Guilt

When Jesus summons us into the journey of "seeing" the kingdom, he invites us into transformation. As amazing as this journey can be, there is no getting around the fact that with clearer vision comes internal chaos. We began to explore this chaos in the previous chapter, "Disorientation," and here we'll go even deeper. Carl Jung, the founder of analytical psychology, said, "There is no coming to consciousness without pain," and this applies to the cultural identity path of a white Christian. An increased consciousness of our present and past history ushers in new levels of discomfort.

Identifying the internal chaos that comes with our awakening is an important but challenging exercise. Dr. Brené Brown, a professor of research at the University of Houston's Graduate College of Social Work, explores this process at length in her bestselling book, *Daring Greatly*. She says that some of the most common words used to describe the array of feelings evoked in times like this are *embarrassment, guilt, humiliation,* and *shame*. While it's possible that all of the above apply, she asserts that it's important to focus on two words from that list: *shame* and *guilt*.

Brown believes that the difference between these two words is far more than semantics. *Guilt* can be a positive and helpful motivator in a person's quest for transformation, but shame rarely produces healthy outcomes. She has done extensive research on shame, and here is the definition that emerged from her research:

> Shame is the intensely painful feeling or experience of believing that we are flawed and therefore unworthy of love and belonging. Shame is the fear of disconnection—it's the fear that something we've done or failed to do, an ideal that we've not lived up to, or a goal that we've not accomplished makes us unworthy of connection. I'm not worthy or good enough for love, belonging, or connection. I'm unlovable. I don't belong.[1]

I resonate with her description of shame for a number of reasons, but the most relevant to this book is the way she links shame to a sense of identity. When people think they're too flawed to be worthy, valuable, or lovable, they've crossed into a new realm of identity formation. This is no longer the quest to just reject bad actions, behaviors, and histories; instead, it opens up the possibility of rejecting their very personhood.

This is why Brown contends that shame is a poor tool for instigating transformation, despite the widespread belief that it's helpful for keeping people in line. She believes it's not only wrong to use shame to motivate people but also dangerous. Her research suggests that it's virtually impossible to correlate shame with positive outcomes of any type, as there are no data to support that shame supports good behavior.[2] Instead shame is more likely to cause destructive and hurtful behaviors than it is to open up solutions. When we're filled with shame, we tend to engage in self-destructive behaviors such as addiction, violence, aggression, depression, eating disorders, and bullying.[3]

Guilt, on the other hand, has all kinds of potential to yield positive behaviors. Brown says it like this:

> When we apologize for something we've done, make amends, or change a behavior that doesn't align with our values, guilt—not shame—is most often the driving force. We feel guilty when we hold up something we've done or failed to do against our values and find they don't match up. It's an uncomfortable feeling, but

one that's helpful. The psychological discomfort, something similar to cognitive dissonance, is what motivates meaningful change. Guilt is just as powerful as shame, but its influence is positive, while shame's is destructive. In fact, in my research I found that shame corrodes the very part of us that believes we can change and do better.[4]

At a personal level, I have found this distinction between shame and guilt to be an important and helpful resource for the cultural identity journey. It's impossible to have your eyes opened to the history of race in our country without experiencing "psychological discomfort" and "cognitive dissonance," both terms that Brown uses in her description above. When the feelings come, we can choose how we will process and internally categorize them.

One option is to go to a place of shame. When we do, we create a story not about what we have done or witnessed but about who we *are*. Shame makes allowance for us to wallow in self-pity and to sink into a hole sustained by a looped message that broadcasts some combination of "I am bad/unlovable/stupid/unworthy/unredeemable." Nobody can survive in a shame spiral for long, so unhealthy coping mechanisms quickly surface. Sometimes a person who feels shame resorts to shaming others. Sometimes a person who feels shame disassociates from his whiteness, as Jeremy did in the opening story. Sometimes a person who feels shame becomes numb and simply shuts down her willingness or ability to receive any additional revelation.

The other option is to embrace guilt as an uncomfortable but meaningful source of growth. Brown says that the majority of shame researchers and clinicians agree that the difference between shame and guilt is best understood as the difference between "I *am* bad" and "I *did* something bad."[5] As we are on the cultural identity journey, we might tweak this difference to be understood as "I *am* bad" and "I *have seen* something that is bad." When we recognize the building blocks of race—the ideology of white supremacy, the narrative of racial difference, ongoing systemic oppression, etc.—we must learn to avoid falling into a shame spiral and instead appropriate the guilt of our discoveries in a way that yields healthy outcomes.

The quest in this stage is to find a way to awaken to the painful truths that come with the journey from blindness to sight, while at the same time not being overcome by shame. I propose that the primary practice to learn is that of lament.

The Confusion Around Lament

I recently participated in a two-day retreat with some Christian leaders from around the country, and every attendee was significantly involved in the work of justice. The gathering was multiethnic, and it was a sacred time together. The agenda was loose, and the topic of conversation shifted as different groups shared burdens they were carrying. One of the tender and transparent moments came when some of the leaders of color who work in all-white organizations shared about navigating that world. Most of them had been recruited to work in atmospheres where they could provide direction for greater levels of diversity and equity, but they often found that their place of employment was as racially stressful as what they experienced in the outside world—or more so.

As the conversation came to a climax, one of the white leaders asked if he could say something. "It breaks my heart to hear of the experiences you all have had in these primarily white organizations, and I'm thankful for your transparency in sharing. I guess I'm seeking some advice, since I work in an organization that probably has some of the very same challenges. I believe we're sincere in wanting to move forward on these initiatives, but I fear we're creating the same type of difficult environment as you're talking about now. So I guess I'm asking, what am I supposed to do?"

As he asked this, I couldn't help but smile. "What am I supposed to do?" seems to be the universal question for white people in the process of awakening. I certainly wasn't judging him for asking it; that question had defined a large part of my own journey. But it was a fresh reminder that most of us react to the initial experience of racial brokenness by searching for an immediate fix. For cultural reasons that go beyond what we tend to comprehend, our instinct is to go right into problem-solving mode.

I understood why he asked it, and I appreciated his desire to improve the organization he led. He had directed his question to the leaders who had shared about working in all-white organizations, so it was theirs to answer. They looked at each other to see who would volunteer to be the spokesperson, and their expressions confirmed that they were all thinking the same thing. One of them finally answered: "What we would ask for you to do is lament."

"Lament?" A furrowed brow showed how confused the question asker was by that answer. He had expected a more concrete answer, so he probed for further clarification. "We've been talking about centuries of oppression that has affected every system, and all you want me to do is lament? I apologize if I'm being slow to get this, but it seems to me that lament is an insufficient prescription to a major problem. Even if we lament, we still need to do something to change all of this, right? Lament isn't going to make my organization become the kind of place for you to work, is it?"

His followup question was understandable. We can't become awakened to the problems of race and then fail to do anything actionable—and nobody in that gathering would have suggested otherwise. Yet, on another level, the incredulousness he showed revealed both a sociological and a theological deficit. Those of us who grew up immersed in white American Christianity often have an anemic understanding of lament, so we fail to understand why it's such a critical part of the reconciliation process.

The Anatomy of Lament

In the Old Testament times, lament was required yet also had to be learned (2 Samuel 1:18). So what is lament?

One of the best books on this topic is *Prophetic Lament*, a study of the book of Lamentations by Dr. Soong-Chan Rah. He launched a church in the Boston area and pastored it for a decade before taking on the position of associate professor of church growth and evangelism at North Park Theological Seminary in Chicago. In the introduction of his book he relies heavily on Old Testament scholar Claus Westermann, who suggests that the Hebrew poetic material of the Bible falls into two broad categories: *praise* and *lament*. Whereas praise poems express worship for the good things God has done, laments are prayers of petition arising out of need. Lament in the Bible is a liturgical response to the reality of suffering and engages God in the context of pain and trouble.[6]

The dichotomy between these two is the basis of Rah's book, and he contended that the modern American church has over-elevated *praise*, which he called *triumphalistic*. Churches that are triumphalistic share a set of common characteristics: they elevate stories of success, gravitate toward narratives of exceptionalism (a view that sees America as inherently different from other nations, with a unique mission to transform the world), emphasize problem solving, and are marked by a can-do attitude backed by a belief that human effort and positive thinking can conquer the big problems we face.

Though there are some redemptive themes in the triumphalistic approach, its dark side is its inability to grasp lament. Rah says it like this:

> The crying out to God in lament over a broken history is often set aside in favor of a triumphalistic narrative. We are too busy patting ourselves on the back over the problem-solving abilities of the triumphant American church to cry out to God in lament.[7]

> American culture tends to hide the stories of guilt and shame
> and seeks to elevate stories of success . . . which results in amnesia
> about a tainted history. The reality of a shameful history under-
> mines the narrative of exceptionalism, so it must remain hidden.[8]

Rah's book has been a helpful tool for me, not only for understanding lament but also for understanding why large sections of the American church seem imbalanced in their theology. While I can appreciate the importance of praise and celebration, I also see the damage that flows from an insufficient emphasis on lament. Suffering, tragedy, oppression, and pain are everyday realities for most of the earth's citizens, and an inability to cry out and grasp for the presence of God in the midst of that suffering is a recipe for hollow spirituality.

Rah's book has also helped me make some important connections between shame, lament, and the cultural identity journey. The praise vs. lament dichotomy shows us why the dominant-culture church often moves quickly toward denial when faced with its historical sins of racial oppression. The process of unearthing our painful history of racial oppression inevitably creates space for guilt and shame, which make human beings uncomfortable. Without a theology to support lament, we become paralyzed in the search for balance and often turn back to the triumphalist narrative as a crutch.

Rah references Brown to underscore this point, effectively bridging shame and lament. When speaking of the inability of the dominant culture to have honest conversations about race, Brown says, "You cannot have that conversation without shame, because you cannot talk about race without talking about privilege. And when people start talking about privilege, they get paralyzed by shame."[9]

So one of the primary reasons American Christians (white, in particular) are unable to deal with the shame stage of the cultural identity journey is we have a feeble lament theology. We're conditioned to celebrate those who experience success and triumph while screening out the message of those who suffer. We too often become "one who sings songs to a heavy heart" (Proverbs 25:20). We've been groomed to search for quick and easy answers to complex problems, and we rarely have the ability to appreciate the act of crying out to God in brokenness and pain.

A City on Fire

One event that rattled the city of Chicago and brought the need for lament to the forefront was the 2015 release of a video from the dashboard camera of a police cruiser that recorded the shooting of teenager Laquan McDonald. Videos of the shootings of unarmed civilians often exacerbate the divide between the white community and certain communities of color, but the pervasiveness of abuse in this episode left our city in a nearly universal state of shock, anger, and sadness.

The video shows a teenager stumbling erratically down a busy street at ten o'clock at night, appearing to be under the influence of some kind of substance. He was also in possession of a three-inch pocketknife, and you can hear the officers shouting at him to drop it. But instead of dropping it, McDonald began heading in the other direction and was then shot as he walked away from the officers. In contradiction to this, the police report claimed that McDonald had verbally threatened the officers first, and the police use of lethal force without provocation served as the first major offense.

Shooting a teenager from behind was bad enough, but what happened next is what made the killing seem cold blooded. After watching McDonald collapse after the first shot, the officer shot him an additional fifteen times, expending the capacity of the semiautomatic firearm. McDonald may have survived the first gunshot, but he had no chance after the second onslaught.

Once the sixteen shots were fired, the scene moves as if in slow motion. Many who've watched the video have felt helpless at the chilling display of a young man dying alone. No one came to his aid or checked on his status as he lay there. Not one person showed even a modicum of interest in this precious child of God as he breathed his final breath. Like the blood of Abel crying out from the ground, McDonald's blood screamed for justice.

Fuel was poured on the fire when it was discovered that a multilayer conspiracy had covered up evidence for more than thirteen months. This was the straw that broke the proverbial camel's back, as it exposed a system of justice failing on all levels. Members of the Chicago Police Department, who are employed to serve and protect, had chosen to tamper with evidence to protect one of their own. The Cook County State Attorney's Office, which was tasked with bringing cases of negligence like this to light, turned a blind eye. The Office of the Mayor, tasked with overseeing the police department, failed to take action of any kind until a whistleblower exposed it. And it certainly didn't dispel perceptions of conspiracy as the coverup overlapped with the political season in which Mayor Rahm Emanuel was running for reelection.

McDonald's death shook Chicago, and it was tragic no matter how one looks at it. But for a time it snapped the city out of its collective slumber. To me, this was most evident in the white church of Chicago, which historically had been silent during eras of racial unrest. White pastors traditionally fear talking about racism from the pulpit, as there is a predictable set of adversarial responses that tend to follow. But something about the undisputable nature of this crime broke through the code of silence. The fact that so many witnessed both the egregious act of the individual officer and the systemic failure of the justice system created a temporary window for honest discussion.

This led to a number of good and important conversations for me. I heard from more white pastor friends wanting to talk about race after the release of the video than I'd heard from over my entire ministerial career. The driving question behind each conversation wasn't a surprise: "I've seen with my own eyes the ways racism is still alive and active. My congregation has seen it with their own eyes as well. We're canceling our normal programs this Sunday to talk about it. But I don't know what to say. What are we supposed to do?"

In every case, I encouraged the pastors to focus on one word: *lament*. I encouraged them to reflect on some questions for their congregations, questions I was also asking of myself. For example, could we lament not only for the loss of McDonald's life but also the loss of the tens of thousands of others killed in the name of race? Could we lament the ideology of white superiority that set the stage for injustices in the first place? Could we lament for the ways our churches had perpetuated racial ideologies, often inadvertently? Could we lament the limitations and blind spots in our theology? Could we lament that we live in a manner that leaves us so disconnected and segregated from the suffering in many communities of color? Could we lament that until we watched the video, we denied that mistreatment was happening?

I found that while my pastor friends were open to considering these questions, the theme of lament seemed insufficient to them. Their reaction reminded me of the previously mentioned young white leader who was incredulous about lament being a response to inequalities: "We've been talking about centuries of oppression . . . and all you want me to do is lament?"

During this season, it became abundantly clear that the dichotomy between a triumphalist and lament approach to church is more than an interesting theological exercise; it has a tremendous impact on how we process pain and suffering in the world. When we're under the influence of triumphalism, we search for "success" in virtually every circumstance, so when a societal problem surfaces, it must be fixed so we can feel a sense of achievement. Therefore an unresolved problem poses a threat. We don't know how to manage the dissonance created by the unsolvable problem, and we struggle to understand the nervous energy created by that tension.

Lament, on the other hand, doesn't function according to the rules of success. It sees suffering not as a problem to be solved but as a condition to be mourned. Lament doesn't see the power of salvation as being in the hands of the oppressors; instead it cries out to God for deliverance from the grip of injustice. Lament is a guttural cry and a longing for God's intervention. It recognizes, as the psalmist so eloquently stated, that hope is found not in chariots and in horses but in God alone (Psalm 20:7).

This contrast points to one of the many reasons lament can be a gift to the white church in particular, if we can just receive it. Lament grants us the freedom to no longer view success as the only viable outcome. Lament gives us permission to admit that we aren't capable of fixing (and may have been part of causing) the problems we've suddenly become awakened to. Lament gives us resources to sit in the tension of suffering and pain without going to a place of shame or self-hate. Lament allows us to acknowledge the limitations of human strength and to look solely to the power of God instead.

A Multicultural Funeral

Lament can take on a variety of forms, and the most helpful image of lament within my community at River City is a funeral. Rah suggested that this form of lament most clearly shaped the Old Testament book of Lamentations: "This opening cry of desolation acknowledges that Lamentations occurs in the context of tragedy. The city has died and the people must respond with lament. . . . Lamentations serves as 'an outpouring of grief for a loss that has already occurred, with no expectation of reversing that loss.'"[10]

This image is both simple and powerful, and I've found it to be a helpful resource for white Christians who are trying to grasp lament at a practical level, particularly in times of distress. When my pastor friends were looking for ways to integrate lament into their services after the release of the video of McDonald's shooting, we emphasized treating services like funerals. This proactively prepares the congregation to let go of the temptation so common in the dominant culture:

to go on the hunt for immediate resolutions to the problem of racism—a temptation that can be difficult to curb. The imagery of a funeral creates much-needed boundaries, as no one would attend the funeral of a friend and then try to rally a group for an immediate problem-solving session. Rah made this point definitively:

> Lament is honesty before God and each other. If something has truly been declared dead, there is no use in sugarcoating that reality. To hide from suffering and death would be an act of denial. If an individual would deny the reality of death during a funeral, friends would justifiably express concern over the mental health of that individual. In the same way, should we not be concerned over a church that lives in denial over the reality of death in our midst?
>
> Our nation's tainted racial history reflects a serious inability to deal with reality. Something has died and we refuse to participate in the funeral. We refuse to acknowledge the lamenters who sing the songs of suffering in our midst.[11]

Lament has been an important resource for River City when we've needed to create spaces that can be occupied by members across the spectrum of privilege and oppression. We've learned the hard way that a community can fracture when there are no clear expectations of those who are shaped by a triumphalist/success narrative as they attempt to enter into a space of lament with those not bound by that set of rules. Those who are already familiar with the spirit of lament go quickly to a place of mourning and suffering, but those who aren't familiar with it either try to fix things or even challenge the very premise of the suffering. However, lamenting by setting the atmosphere of a funeral, the posture of the entire congregation changes. We are then able to enter sober mourning and divert our attention from solving a problem to fixing our gaze on the character of God.

Those lessons helped me gravitate to the image of a multicultural funeral, and that was the image I passed on to my pastor friends during that time of turmoil in Chicago. Let me put it in the form of a question: If a beloved member of a household is killed, isn't it assumed that the entire family will be at the funeral service to mourn the loss? How odd would it be if one of the family members didn't show up? How conspicuous would her absence be?

That's the problem we're facing in the American church right now. The funeral services are happening, and people of color are being mourned over. But where are the white members of the family? Why are we not at the funeral? How conspicuous is our absence? Who is noticing our absence? Is it everyone but us?

Putting Lament into Practice

Because most of us are unacquainted with lament, it can feel daunting to practice it when the necessity arises. Though I understand the insecurity many of us feel, I believe this insecurity erects an unnecessary obstacle. Lament is meant to be accessible to each of us, regardless of where we are in our journey.

A number of biblical stories and psalms have inspired my understanding of lament over the years, and one of the most enduringly helpful is in the book of Esther: Mordecai adopts his orphaned cousin, Hadassah (Esther), and raises her as if she were his own daughter. He refuses the governmental decree to prostrate himself before Haman, a vizier in the Persian Empire under King Xerxes. In retaliation, Haman instigates a plot to kill all the Jews of Persia. Haman convinces the king to sign off on this execution order (Esther 3:10), and when Mordecai hears the news he responds with lament: "When Mordecai learned of all that had been done, he tore his clothes, put on sackcloth and ashes, and went out into the city, wailing loudly and bitterly" (Esther 4:1).

The raw simplicity of Mordecai's response gives us a clear picture of how to lament: we posture ourselves before God to wail, cry, and mourn. To lament is to acknowledge the pain that we aren't home and that this world is too often marked by evil and injustice. To lament is to ask God the haunting questions "Where are you? What are you doing? How long must we wait?"

To ask these questions is not to doubt or challenge God. Instead, as Dr. Dan Allender eloquently states,

> It is crucial to comprehend a lament is as far from complaining or grumbling as a search is from aimless wandering. A grumbler has already reached a conclusion, shut down all desire and postures with questions that are barely concealed accusations. . . . A lament involves even deeper emotion because a lament is truly asking, seeking, and knocking to comprehend the heart of God. A lament involves the energy to search, not to shut down the quest for truth. It is passion to ask, rather than to rant and rave with already reached conclusions. A lament uses the language of pain, anger, and confusion and moves toward God.[12]

I've also learned from Mordecai's response that lament is identification with the pain of the people. Though Haman's actions affected Mordecai personally, the primary thrust of his lament was the threat toward the Jews of Persia. Their lives were in serious danger, and the recognition of this compelled him to wail loudly and bitterly before God.

This last point has particular relevance for the cultural identity of white people. One of the most common concerns I've heard from white Christians regarding this kind of lament is that they feel sheepish doing it, especially when the injustice they're lamenting doesn't affect them the way it does many people of color. While I'm grateful for the self-awareness they show through this observation, I challenge the premise that privilege should stop us from following in the footsteps of Mordecai (and others).

A couple of passages from the apostle Paul remind us of the importance of solidarity. In Romans 12:15, we're told to "mourn with those who mourn," and in 1 Corinthians 12:26, Paul says, "If one part [of the body] suffers, every part suffers with it." In other words, we are not only allowed to lament in solidarity with those who are suffering, we are *commanded* to.

That's why solidarity around suffering is one of the most important actions in our cultural identity journey. When our sisters and brothers of color are suffering—or worse, being killed—it's an absolute imperative that we suffer alongside them. We need to show them that we see them and that we see their suffering. We need to show them that we see the injustice behind the suffering and that we lament its ongoing presence. We need to be locked arm in arm with our extended family, crying out to God in a collective spirit of lament.

Moving Forward

Carl Jung wrote, "There is no coming to consciousness without pain." An authentic cultural identity journey always results in seeing the kingdom of God in new ways, and with those new discoveries come new challenges. An increased understanding of our present and of our history ushers in new levels of discomfort. Learning to respond in a healthy way to the internal chaos aroused by our awakening is an important step forward.

Shame is one of the stages of racial awakening, and it's understandable how feelings of guilt can take on a life of their own. But shame is an ineffective tool for instigating the transformation of our lives Jesus seeks. Shame creates a story that's not about what we've witnessed, discovered, or been complicit in, but about whom each of us *is* as a person. This story then pulls us in the opposite direction of a Christ-led, cultural identity journey. When we fall into a shame spiral, we give in to coping mechanisms that further disconnect us from the pursuit of reconciliation and justice.

Instead we need to discover the deep spiritual resources that come with the practice of lament. We need to learn to see the side of God's character that sees the misery of his people and that hears the cries of the suffering (see Exodus 3:7; Psalm 10:17). We need to become conscious of our instinct to look for quick fixes and to avoid the full weight of the suffering.

Self-Righteousness

One of the most transformative things that happened to me during my Willow Creek days occurred long before I was a candidate to come on staff there. Back in my early twenties, when I first became heavily involved, I decided I was ready to become a member. Joining a church felt like a very grown-up thing to do.

However, when I looked into the membership process, I discovered that it included an intensive one-on-one interview with someone from the church. While the high bar the church set for membership was inspiring, I was intimidated. I wondered what I might be asked in the interview. And I wondered if my growing faith would stand up under the lights.

Despite my insecurities, I worked up the courage to move forward. I signed up to be interviewed by Rick Shurtz, one of the young-adult pastors. Because he had already interacted with me in a ministry in which we both served, he had a good sense of where he wanted the conversation to go. He opened our time with a prayer and then asked me to share my salvation story.

I told him some of my testimony: As the son of a pastor, I was familiar with altar calls and had given my life to Christ many times as a young person. I also confessed deep regret about mistakes I made during my high school and college years, and I acknowledged that some of my behaviors flew in the face of a God who had extended so much love to me. I then assured Rick that I was aware of the gravity of my sin and that I was set on making amends to God. I told him I would prove first to God and then to Willow Creek that God had not made a mistake when he extended me the gift of salvation. I would make up for lost time, I told him, and I would make the church proud if they included me as part of their membership roster.

I'll never forget how serious Rick got in that moment. He shut his notebook and took a moment to compose his thoughts. As we sat there in silence, I became convinced that he was going to tell me I was disqualified based on my uneven track record. But that's not what he did. Instead he said, "Daniel, let's not worry about passing this interview. You're already approved to be a member. You're going to be a fantastic addition to the Willow Creek community. I'm not concerned with any of that. What I'd like to do is spend the rest of our time talking about grace."

I was surprised to hear him say that, but also relieved. I had been preoccupied with finding out if I would be accepted by the "in" group, and the security of knowing that I was freed me to engage openly for the rest of the conversation.

Rick thanked me for sharing so openly and then lovingly told me he wanted to explore some self-righteousness he had detected in my story. All I could think was, *Whoa, self-righteousness?* I didn't know what he meant by that, but I was pretty sure I didn't want to be associated with it. I also knew Rick was a caring and compassionate man who wouldn't say something unless he thought it would benefit me. So I geared up and invited him to continue.

Rick explained what he meant by self-righteousness and shared his view on the big difference between being accepted into the family of God based on the record of Jesus and having an internal pressure to prove that my record was worthy of acceptance. He talked about how big the difference is between embracing the gift of forgiveness without strings and feeling I was forever chained to the mistakes I'd made. He drew a sharp distinction between deriving a sense of righteousness from my identity in Christ and deriving a sense of righteousness from my deeds.

As he shared his thoughts, I was having an out-of-body experience. At some level, what he was saying was not new at all; I had heard presentations of the gospel at every stage of my upbringing. On the other hand, his description of grace, repentance, and identity in Christ was so beautiful that I burst into tears. I hadn't realized the degree to which I had taken on the burden of self-righteousness, and I felt an unbelievable release when I allowed the good news of the gospel of grace to wash over my soul.

This was a pivotal moment in my spiritual life—the first time I saw the power of self-righteousness and understood how to combat it with the gospel. Little did I know I would need to learn it all over again in my cultural identity journey.

The One-Degree Rule

In aviation, there's a principle called the one-degree rule: a tiny error in direction can make a major difference in the final destination of a flight. If you're one degree off for a mile, that means a ninety-foot miss; and if the trip is sixty miles, the plane will miss its target by a full mile. If your direction is one degree off from New York to Los Angeles, you end up being fifty miles off course.

When it comes to identifying extreme forms of self-righteousness, the one-degree rule isn't necessary. After all, it doesn't require high levels of discernment to recognize when a highly judgmental person has gone off course, right? But what about when self-righteousness presents itself as small and seemingly insignificant? Do we notice it then? Do we even care?

Jesus' clearest teaching on unchecked self-righteousness comes in the parable of the prodigal son (or actually *sons*). The father in the parable, who represents God, has two sons. The younger of the two demands his inheritance and then proceeds to squander all his wealth in "wild living" (Luke 15:13). He eventually hits rock bottom when he's competing with pigs for their food. At that point, he finally comes to his senses. (Incidentally, "coming to our senses" is a very effective phrase for describing conversion.)

By then, the younger prodigal has given up any expectation that he will be accepted back as a son, but he knows that his father is a man of compassion, so he hopes to be received as a servant. He begins the long trip home and is spotted from far off by the hopeful father. Breaking every Middle Eastern protocol for a dignified male, the father runs full speed to welcome the prodigal home.

The over-the-top reception that the younger son got often steals the spotlight, yet the tale of the older brother is every bit as significant. His story is a case study for the one-degree rule: though he dutifully followed the house rules, his obedience wasn't flowing from a grateful heart. Instead he was driven by his own selfish agenda. Though this distinction was difficult to detect from the outside, it eventually showed itself in the cumulative toll that it took on his soul. By the time it bubbled to the surface, the elder brother was marked by a combination of anger, joylessness, judgment, and most sadly, an inability to internalize the love of the Father (Luke 15:28-30).

I appreciate this parable because it normalizes the ways self-righteousness plays a role in shaping the identity trajectory for each us. Like the older brother, we all have moments along the way when we rediscover that just because our identity *can* be rooted in the love of the Father doesn't mean it always is. Every time we base our identity on anything else—such as our own accomplishments, achievements, and/or good behaviors—we begin to go down a path strikingly similar to that of the older brother. Even one degree of self-righteousness is enough to knock us off course, which can send us far off course in the long run. This is true in many arenas of the spiritual life, and it's especially true in the journey of cultural identity development.

The True Test of Self-Righteousness

How do we detect when we're in the self-righteousness stage? This parable from Jesus gives us some very direct answers:

> To some who were confident of their own righteousness and looked down on everyone else, Jesus told this parable: "Two men went up to the temple to pray, one a Pharisee and the other a tax collector. The Pharisee stood by himself and prayed: 'God, I thank you that I am not like other people—robbers, evildoers, adulterers—or even like this tax collector. I fast twice a week and give a tenth of all I get.'
>
> "But the tax collector stood at a distance. He would not even look up to heaven, but beat his breast and said, 'God, have mercy on me, a sinner.'
>
> "I tell you that this man, rather than the other, went home justified before God. For all those who exalt themselves will be humbled, and those who humble themselves will be exalted." (Luke 18:9-14)

Though this parable is hard-hitting, its straightforwardness has long been a gift to me. Jesus wasted no time making his point, and in his opening line he laid bare what unveiled self-righteousness looks like: "To some who were confident of their own righteousness and looked down on everyone else, Jesus told this parable."

The parable's subject is a Pharisee, and critique of him begins with the way he (and others) placed confidence in his "own righteousness." The Pharisees had very specific categories for right living that need not obscure the universal application of what Jesus said here. As human beings, we all consistently do the same thing. We create and recreate our own categories of right living, which serve as failed attempts to prop up an established sense of identity. One's educational level, racial background, political affiliation, commitment to a social cause, abstinence from a certain activity, adherence to a certain set of doctrines, or any other combination can be the criteria. Our modern tendencies reveal that we aren't that different from this first-century Pharisee that got the unenviable job of serving as Jesus' illustration.

After showing the danger of placing our confidence in our own righteousness, Jesus moved on to make evident the telltale, irrefutable sign of self-righteousness: the Pharisee "looked down on everyone else."

The brilliance of this statement first popped out at me when I was working on my doctoral thesis. I was required to study a particular field from the social sciences as part of my thesis, so I chose to study social identity theory. This theory relates to the cultural identity themes of this book in that it addresses the ways in which people perceive and categorize themselves in society. Of particular interest is the way a person's sense of identity is shaped by *in-group* and *out-group* association. At its most basic level, an in-group is a social group to which an individual feels he or she belongs, and an out-group is a social group with which an individual doesn't identify. The in-group we associate with becomes an important source of pride and self-esteem, and it gives us a sense of belonging. However, in an attempt to bolster that sense of belonging, human beings tend to belittle, discriminate against, and hold prejudices against the out-group we don't belong to.

Hundreds of experiments have been done on in-group/out-group dynamics, and I explored many of them for my thesis project. One that's often referred to in the study of social categorization wasn't a formal experiment, yet it verifies common findings. In 1968, the day after the assassination of Martin Luther King Jr., a teacher named Jane Elliot tried something in a schoolroom in Iowa, and the results were strikingly similar to what Jesus addressed in Luke 18.

Elliot focused on the problems of racial prejudice by dividing her third-grade class into groups on the basis of eye color.[1] She allowed the "better" blue-eyed children to discriminate against the brown-eyed children. Within minutes, the blue-eyed children sadistically ridiculed their unfortunate classmates, calling them stupid and shunning them in the playground during recess. Then she flipped the situation, and the brown-eyed children exacted the same punishments on their blue-eyed classmates.

As I studied this quasi-experiment as well as dozens like it, I realized they confirmed what Jesus had directly addressed two millennia before. With his parable on self-righteousness, he used the language of *in-group* and *out-group* long before modern psychology popularized it. That Pharisee exhibited all the findings of social identity theory when he divided his world into the binary categories of "good" people and "bad" people. He was establishing a pseudo sense of identity by organizing his standing based on his membership in the in-group. And he bolstered that standing by discriminating against the out-group, which he identified by name in his prayer: "God, I thank you that I am not like other people—robbers, evildoers, adulterers—or even like this tax collector" (Luke 18:11).

We all do this, and the criteria we use for dividing the world into good/bad, in/out can be as diverse as humanity itself. Jonathan Martin, one of my favorite preachers, tells a story of going to a pair of pastor's conferences on back-to-back weekends and witnessing this division of people into the good/bad binary on opposite ends of the spectrum. The first conference was of a more conservative persuasion, and this group split the world into those who held a traditional view of marriage and those that held another view. Though the conference was supposed to address a wide range of issues, participants were so fixated by the in/out of that one issue that it overwhelmed the rest of the agenda.

On the very next weekend he went to a pastor's conference that was of a more liberal persuasion, and the same thing happened but with a different set of values. Within this group he found a fixation with those who were concerned about environmental issues and those who were not. They made constant jokes about SUV driving and gas guzzlers, and they seemed unable to take anyone seriously that wasn't at the same level of environmental "enlightenment."

I'm not minimizing the importance of holding to a personal opinion or conviction on a topic. Scripture is clear that we as Christ's followers are to align our beliefs with the teachings of God rather than conform to the ways of the world. The problem comes when we subtly shift from appropriate conviction to sinful comparing. The Pharisee in this parable was sinfully comparing in order to separate himself from the people he judged to be unworthy of God's love and favor. Self-righteousness points to a deep foundational reality. It has to do with identity and how we pursue an inner sense of belonging. It has to do with our sense of being right with God, with the world, and with our neighbors.

When we allow our sense of belonging to be shaped by the in/out, us/them binary of good and bad, we fall into what entrapped the Pharisee. We exert inordinate amounts of energy trying to prove that we belong in the good group (with *earning, achieving,* and *validating* as ways of proving it). We also can't help but look down on those that are in the other group with judgment and at times even disdain.

Good White People, Bad White People

Dr. Robin DiAngelo, whose work on white fragility we explored in chapter five, is also helpful when discussing self-righteousness. Though she approaches this topic from a secular perspective, it's intriguing how clearly her ideas intersect with Jesus' teachings:

> For white people, their identities rest on the idea of racism as about good or bad people, about moral or immoral singular acts, and if we're good, moral people we can't be racist—we don't engage in those acts.... In large part, white fragility—the defensiveness, the

fear of conflict—is rooted in this good/bad binary. If you call someone out, they think to themselves, "What you just said was that I am a bad person, and that is intolerable to me." It's a deep challenge to the core of our identity as good, moral people.[2]

There's a lot in this quote, so let's clarify it. It's very difficult to recognize the presence of something unhealthy within us if it isn't overtly obvious (moral or immoral singular acts). To survive the pressure that self-awareness creates, we develop defense mechanisms in relation to contradictory acts.

One powerful defense mechanism is to judge only what is most behaviorally observable in our lives. However, when we live like this, we protect ourselves from the weight of genuine self-examination and all its implications. For example, if we allowed ourselves to see how deep the roots of greed go into our hearts, we would make changes in how we spend money and what we do with prized possessions. If we instead focus on a singular moral act, such as a financial contribution to a charity, it's easier to ignore the countless ways in which we take rather than give.

Most of us find it difficult to be at peace with ourselves when we don't feel that we're good, moral people, as DiAngelo aptly phrased it. If we're challenged on this, an immediate instinct to protect our idea of who we are comes into play so we can continue functioning. This is part of what makes us so fragile; something is fragile when it can't handle weight or pressure without breaking. Her observation is that because white people's gauge of being good and moral is critical to their sense of identity, there's an inherent fragility that can't take the weight of difficult inner realities, such as the presence of racism (no matter how subtle it is).

With this quote from DiAngelo in one hand and the teachings of Jesus in the other, I'd like to draw out a handful of important links between self-righteousness, cultural identity, and the dismantling of racism:

- Self-righteousness undermines healthy identity development, making the fifth stage particularly important in the cultural identity journey.

- Self-righteousness undermines our ability to dismantle the system of racism, making this a particularly important stage for those who want to be active participants in Jesus' redemptive work.

- The cure for self-righteousness is found in repentance, making repentance a particularly important spiritual discipline for the cultural identity journey.

Self-righteousness undermines healthy identity development. The Pharisee split the world into binary categories of good/bad and in/out. So do most white people. According to DiAngelo's words above, we too often allow our identity to "rest on the idea" that there are good white people with whom we long to be associated and bad white people whom we choose to shun. *yep.*

I see this tendency in almost every white person seeking greater levels of racial awareness, and my own story is no different. In fact, with the benefit of hindsight, I see that this was the most formative stage of my cultural identity journey. My most intensified awakening overlapped with the period of my most intensified battle with self-righteousness. I didn't have the awareness to classify it as self-righteousness at the time, but any objective person who applied the tests of social identity theory would have.

The first manifestation of self-righteousness, according to Jesus' parable, is that we place too much confidence in our own sense of rightness. Whereas the Pharisee did this by drawing a circle around the way his group attended to the detailed obedience of the Torah, I did it by drawing a circle around those I saw as being awake to racial justice. Consistent with classic in-group/out-group behavior, I worked hard to prove that I belonged to this group that I deemed to be awakened to race and active to address it. So I became borderline obsessive about achieving the approval of those whose opinion on race mattered to me. This included just about every person of color I knew and white people I admired who were doing the work of reconciliation and justice. I would brag, pontificate, share tales of my exploits, and do just about anything I could think of to prove to them that I was an enlightened contributor to the movement of racial reconciliation. I was as textbook as they come.

According to Jesus, the second manifestation of self-righteousness, as well as its telltale sign, is looking down on those who live contrary to the values of our in-group. It was obvious to me who belonged to the out-group category of *bad* people: every white person that didn't care about racial justice. I took some sort of twisted pride in distancing myself from those I deemed as unenlightened, and I thought this enhanced my standing as one of the *good* white people who got it. I eventually discovered how dangerous this self-righteousness is and made a commitment to find a way out.

I want to be sure to emphasize the threat self-righteousness poses to healthy identity development. As explored at multiple points, we are our best and most redeemed self when our identity is rooted in our status as beloved children of God. When our sense of belonging rests on anything else, we lose touch with that redeemed self. As important as the racial awakening journey is, we must remain aware of the ways we form an evolved sense of identity based on group identity. We are drawn to prove that we belong to the good/in-group, and we are tempted to judge those in the bad/out-group. This has a major impact on the development of our cultural identity journey, and the faster we can spot the presence of self-righteousness the better.

Self-righteousness undermines our ability to dismantle the system of racism. DiAngelo highlights another very important idea when she alludes to the relationship between cultural identity and the nature of racism: "For white people, their identities rest on the idea of racism as about good or bad people, about moral or immoral singular acts, and if we're good, moral people we can't be racist—we don't engage in those acts."

My experience suggests that she's right when she says that most white people essentially define racism as being about "moral or immoral singular acts." In other words, we think of racism as an individual person doing or committing an individually bad deed.

If that were all that racism entailed, it wouldn't be difficult to eradicate. We would just need to sequester all the bad people who do bad things and then trust that the world would move back to a state of equality. This would simplify the cultural identity journey as well, and all we'd need to do is ensure that we remain on the side of the "good" white people and avoid anything that implicates us with the "bad" ones.

That is, of course, a naive view of both cultural identity and racism. Racism is far more lethal than a handful of individual actors committing individual immoral acts. A much more holistic way to think of racism comes when we look at it through the lens of the four interlocking facets that we explored in the "Encounter" chapter:

- ◆ Racism reflects a social construct created for the purposes of consolidating white power.

- ◆ Racism is an extension of the ideology of white supremacy, a doctrine that paints white people as inherently superior to people from all other racial groups.

- ◆ A narrative of racial difference was created to support this ideology of white superiority, which measures human value based on proximity to whiteness.

- ◆ The narrative of racial difference—both historically and currently—infects systems and structures, thus perpetuating racial inequality throughout society.

Only when we view racism through all four of these lenses do we appreciate the depth of its power and pervasiveness of its presence.

At this point we begin to grasp the nuanced relationship between self-righteousness, cultural identity, and the dismantling of racism. The flow tends to go something like this: As human beings, we are always battling self-righteousness. We are caught between the pull of building our identity through our own efforts on one side and rooting our identity in the love and grace of the Father on the other.

More specifically, as white people pursuing deeper levels of engagement with cultural identity, we're tempted to bolster our sense of identity through group association. The telltale sign of self-righteousness in everyday identity is drawing a circle around the in-group and pointing a judgmental finger at those in the out-group. In the cultural identity journey, this usually manifests as trying to prove that you belong to the group that "gets" it—or as many in my congregation joke, as being the "cool" white person that's on the side of justice. This inevitably leads to judgment, and at times even scorn, toward those who have the other vices and behaviors.

Finally, self-righteousness undercuts our ability to combat and dismantle racism. Once we've committed to a course of identity formation defined by self-righteousness and self-inclusion in the "good" group, we're susceptible to a watered-down analysis of race. Rather than acknowledging the pervasive way race shapes us all, we look for ways to reduce racism to individual acts of immorality. While this allows us to maintain the illusion of a binary world of good/bad and in/out, it also undercuts our ability to do anything meaningful to combat racism.

The Beauty of Repentance

Once you're able to acknowledge the tendencies to drift toward self-righteousness—and I hope we all are—the obvious question is "How do I move out of the self-righteousness stage?" The answer is found in a single word that's equal parts beautifully simple and frustratingly complex: *repentance.*

First, let's embrace its beautiful simplicity. While many theological squabbles tend to partition the church, repentance is one of those wonderful doctrines that unite believers. Christians of every tradition acknowledge that repentance is the key to God's heart, and we trust that it unleashes God's grace.

We all agree that repentance is a mandatory discipline for breaking free of self-righteousness. This is confirmed in the parable of the prodigal son, as the father begs the older brother to repent of his protest. The father assures him that the entire inheritance is awaiting him, and he needs to come home to receive the gift of God's grace. We also see this in the self-righteous Pharisee (Luke 18). We know that if he would just repent for constructing his identity on his good deeds, he would discover the life-altering joy of having an identity built on the grace and love of God.

So repentance is beautifully simple and straightforward. It is to come home to the Father. It is to confess of our sin and to bask in God's grace. It is to turn away from self-driven efforts to build an identity and to allow the grace and love of God to serve as our foundation.

But as beautifully simple as repentance is—and it truly is—it can also be frustratingly complex. This is especially true when it comes to white Christians' cultural identity journey. In many areas of life, repentance seems to come with relative ease, but there's something different about repentance in regard to race and cultural identity.

I learned this in a very public way. In the previous chapter, I told the story of the shooting of Laquan McDonald. A variety of protests and actions ensued in the wake of the release of the video, and the city was tense. In response, a group of pastors from the South Side, where McDonald had been shot and killed, felt God leading them to plan a citywide event that focused on galvanizing Christians. The vision was built around prayer and social action, and the decision was made to host a prayer vigil on the front steps of the Chicago Police Department headquarters, at Thirty-Fifth and Michigan.

Many Christians from throughout the city attended, and I was humbled to be one of the clergy who was invited to pray. Each pastor was given a different topic to address in prayer, with themes ranging from lament for the loss of life to intercession for greater justice in the police system. The topic assigned to me was repentance, and when it came my turn to pray, it felt necessary to include a prayer of repentance for the ways in which white Christians have been complicit in racism throughout American history.

When the event concluded, I assumed that would be the end of it, but the vigil drew significant interest from across the county. The entire nation was embroiled in racial tension, and the raw footage of McDonald's shooting had put Chicago in the spotlight. As a result, a variety of major news networks attended, including CNN. A CNN reporter called me about an hour after the event and said that a number of the reporters in their studio were talking about how unusual it was to see a white pastor praying about repentance at a Black Lives Matters event. (It was not technically a BLM event, but that was how they portrayed it.) They asked me if I would do a live interview to discuss the topic further.

I felt uneasy about the offer, as it didn't take much discernment to see how much privilege was being extended to me. Twelve women and men of color had eloquently shared important prayers at the vigil, yet CNN was pursuing the one white pastor for an interview. On top of that, I wasn't even one of the organizing pastors, and that made me feel even less qualified to speak.

One of the lessons I've learned in my years at River City is that when navigating complicated racial terrain, it's important not to live in my own head. I believe in the blindness-to-sight paradigm and therefore have little regard for my ability to answer questions alone. So before I replied to CNN, I reached out to a number of mentors as well as the organizers of the event. I told them of my uneasiness with being invited as the only white pastor who had prayed. Each person I spoke to agreed that it was an obvious display of white privilege that confirmed a recurring pattern of white people ignoring the voices of people of color.

Despite that observation, they also strongly believed I should seize the opportunity, agreeing that it was a good way to discuss the issue on a larger platform. They said privilege shouldn't keep me from being faithful to discuss repentance with a national audience. One of my pastor friends gave me the bottom line: "Every black pastor in America says this exact thing from the pulpit every Sunday, but we all know white America isn't going to listen to them. But they just might listen to you."

Things progressed quickly, and I was in the CNN studio the following afternoon. I wasn't given any indication of what we would be talking about or what I would be asked. So I went without an agenda, other than a commitment to do my best to center the conversation on Jesus. That may sound churchy, but it was the truth. I didn't want to perpetuate a view of social action that's detached from Christian faith, and I hoped to bear witness to the gospel. I wasn't sure if I could bring up the name of Jesus, but I was certainly going to try.

It was somewhat shocking and extremely pleasant when the interview began with a full replay of my prayer. I started to feel giddy. I couldn't believe they were airing a prayer on CNN. It was over three minutes long, and they showed it in its entirety, so I couldn't help but let my mind wander a bit. I found myself back in my Pentecostal upbringing, remembering our reverence of those saints that found a way to go public with their faith. We often joked in youth group that if one of us ever talked about Jesus on *Oprah* or could hit the game-winning shot and then bear witness to Christ in our post-game comments, we could retire right then and go straight to heaven. Well, this wasn't Oprah, but CNN wasn't a bad second.

When the video of the prayer finally ended, Brooke Baldwin introduced me and then jumped right in. She began by asking why a white pastor had prayed about repentance at a Black Lives Matter event. Then she gave me an uninterrupted space to share. I talked about the biblical importance of repentance, the centrality of grace, and the need to have the mind of Christ regarding our historical relationship with race.

The interview ended shortly after, and as I walked out of the CNN studio, I felt a deep sense of satisfaction. The segment was seven minutes—an eternity in TV time—and it was saturated with the name of Jesus from beginning to end. I was thrilled about the clear focus on prayer and repentance in the midst of troubling times.

Those feelings of excitement evaporated pretty quickly when I turned on my phone. Social media was blowing up with angry responses to the interview, and the overwhelming majority came from white Christians frustrated with what I'd said. Here's one tweet that summarized the larger body of angry replies: "If you see yourself as a racist, then go ahead and repent for yourself. But don't you dare repent for me. I'm not a racist, and I don't need some white pastor confessing for me."

This wasn't the first time I'd encountered people upset that I had repented for racism. It's something I've done plenty of times, though never on such a large stage. But what happened after CNN was unlike anything I could have predicted. Not only were thousands of white Christians angry with me, but they were diligent in finding my contact information on every social medium on the Internet: Twitter, Facebook, Instagram, YouTube, the River City website. Angry callers even found the phone number for River City and left hundreds of voicemails. Many of them were threatening enough that the Chicago police had to get involved (which was ironic, since I was doing the interview because of police brutality).

I won't risk oversimplifying why so many white Christians responded the way they did. But I walked away convinced that the intersection of repentance and cultural identity and race can be very tricky for white Christians in particular.

I was pretty shaken by the angry responses, and I began to wonder if I was relaying the biblical call to repentance accurately. I went back to Scripture, looking for answers, and found guidance in an unexpected place: a party with Jesus.

In Desperate Need of the Great Physician

Luke 5:27-32 provides a picture for repentance—particularly a picture that addresses self-righteousness. Jesus famously called on Levi the tax collector to leave his old life behind and follow him. Levi indeed became a disciple and eventually took the name Matthew (which means "gift of God").

Shortly after this conversion, it dawned on Levi that while his new life was absolutely amazing, he may have some responsibilities to the friends he'd left behind. Back in his heyday, he'd been known as quite the partier (Luke 5:29), so he figured a party would be a good place to introduce his new group of friends to his old group of friends. Presumably to his delight, not only Jesus was amicable to the idea but also his entire crew of tax collectors.

While the party was a big hit, it also drew the ire of the Pharisees. They were uncomfortable that Jesus so openly associated with sinners, a view that comes as little surprise when we consider the markers of social identity theory. Given the propensity of Pharisees to drift toward self-righteousness, it was predictable that Jesus' choice to commune with those from the out-group was met with confusion.

Their presence creates the backdrop for one of the most important teachings Jesus gave on repentance. In the first publicly recorded question from Pharisees (which seems to intensify its meaning), they ask, "Why do you eat and drink with tax collectors and sinners?" To this, Jesus simply replied, "It is not the healthy who need a doctor, but the sick. I have not come to call the righteous, but sinners to repentance" (Luke 5:30-32).

This single sentence is loaded with meaning, as Jesus aimed his response directly at self-righteousness. Though he didn't technically use the prefix *self* when he said, "I have not come to call the righteous," it is the clear implication, since all followers of Jesus are made righteous through faith in him. What's undoubtedly clear is Jesus' portrayal of self-righteousness as oppositional to his call.

In the passage, Jesus also didn't allude to repentance as having to do with a person's deeds—good or bad. This would have been (and always will be) both confusing and confrontational for anyone oriented to viewing sin through a behavioral grid. In the world of self-righteousness, the only means to prove your worth and develop your identity is by associating with well-behaved people and by avoiding badly behaved people. But if good deeds and bad deeds are no longer the primary markers for belonging, where does that leave repentance?

This leads to the third and most important thing that jumps out from this passage. When Jesus taught on repentance here, he grounded it in a pair of evocative images: sin is likened to being *sick* (as opposed to being classified as bad), and righteousness is likened to being *healthy* (as opposed to being classified as good).

For those seeking union with Christ, the implication is clear. While being a Christian always entails seeking right behavior and avoiding wrong behavior, our vision for transformation is always hampered if this is the limit of our sight. Instead our transformation requires that we first are able to take an accurate appraisal of ourselves. We must embrace the fact that we are far beyond misbehaved or immoral—we are *sick*. A sick person can't cure her condition with hard work or good deeds. The only hope is a cure from the outside. The only hope is Jesus.

Here I see a deeply spiritual connection between repentance in the life of faith and repentance in the cultural identity journey. If most of us approach the development of cultural identity through a self-righteousness grid—and I've done my best to convince you that we do—then there are some dynamics we can assume are happening at an internal level.

First, we can assume that we're drawing most of our cultural identity from a commitment to group membership. We quickly develop a sense of who the in-group is that gets it and who the out-group is that doesn't. Much of our success in the cultural identity journey is therefore determined simply by whether or not we can convince ourselves that we have successfully associated with the in-group.

Second, we can assume that the primary test for group membership is our behavior, our deeds. We intuitively identify a set of behaviors we believe defines the in-group, and we work hard to ascribe to those. We also identify behaviors that mark the out-group—much as the Pharisees did with those who were sexually immoral and financially unscrupulous—and we work hard to avoid these. The successful negotiation of these behaviors is a critical dimension of "rightness." They prove that we belong in the right group and that we have successfully distanced ourselves from the wrong group.

Third, and as a result of the first two, we have a very limited vision of repentance as it applies to the cultural identity journey. While we may respect the fact that bad deeds must still be confessed, our divine imagination is still restricted to behaviors. In the same way that the words of Jesus confused the well-meaning Pharisees, this line often confuses our cultural identity development. Again, "it is not the healthy who need a doctor, but the sick. I have not come to call the righteous, but sinners to repentance."

One amazing thing about this conversation between the Pharisees and Jesus is that they all were striving for the same thing: righteousness. They just had very different visions for how to get there. The Pharisees believed they had to earn their way in and then prove that they belonged. They wanted to convince Jesus that they were already healthy.

Jesus, on the other hand, never asked them to prove their righteousness. He already knew they weren't righteous. And he certainly didn't ask them to portray themselves as healthy. He had already identified them as sick. Ironically, all they needed to do to be righteous was admit they weren't. All they needed to do to become healthy was admit they weren't. The cure was right there.

That's why repentance is such great news for the hungry heart. Once you realize you're sick, you stop trying to act healthy. And you go on the search for the cure. When you discover that the cure was already searching for you, an explosion of gratitude makes sense.

That's why I so regularly and comfortably repent for the sins of white Christians—both for mine and for the sins of my community. It isn't because I think I'm better than everybody else or that I'm trying to prove that some bad white Christians out there need to be chastised. No, I repent all the time because I believe I'm surrounded by the sickness of racism. I see the sickness in the ideology of white supremacy and have no doubt that it has infected me. I see the sickness in the narrative of racial difference and have no doubt it has infected me. I see the sickness of systemic racism and have no doubt that I contribute to it in ways I'm not aware of. I'm surrounded by sickness, and I *am* sick. I am in need of the great Physician. It's the only hope I have to be healthy.

That's also why I see repentance as the single most important spiritual discipline associated with cultural identity development. I would even say that it's the single most important spiritual discipline for finding white liberation. This new vision of repentance blows up the self-righteousness grid and brings forth liberation.

Now we no longer have to base our cultural identity on an association with the good group.

Now we no longer have to base our cultural identity on a rejection of the bad group.

Now we no longer have to worry about proving, earning, or achieving acceptance.

Instead we can acknowledge that we're surrounded by the sickness of racism. And when we expand our definition of repentance to include the intake of toxins from our polluted racial environment, it becomes not only easy but also something we desperately need. We can drop all pretenses, finally, and simply confess our wholesale need for Jesus.

amen

9

Awakening

I recently led a lengthy workshop on white identity with a group of students at an InterVarsity event at a university in Chicago. It was a vibrant conversation, and I left feeling very positive about our interactions. When I was in college, neither my friends nor I were engaging in anything deep regarding faith—and certainly not anything as significant as cultural identity. Yet there was a group of young adults wrestling very seriously with what it means to be a white Christian in our day and age, and it inspired me.

We covered much of the same material as what's in this book and then set aside some time for Q&A and discussion at the end. One of the students, who had clearly been paying attention, put a preface before his final question: "By now I am very clear that I shouldn't ask the question 'What am I supposed to do?'" Everyone laughed, which affirmed that I had covered that point more than enough times. He then asked, "Is there any way to tell if or when we are moving toward authentic awakening? Are there any markers along the road that tell us whether we're going the right direction?"

These are legitimate questions, and they set the stage for what I'd like to explore in this sixth stage: awakening. While I always emphasize the need for white people to seek revelation, knowledge, wisdom, and insight humbly, it's also reasonable to be paying attention to certain markers of progress along the way. This isn't to insinuate that we're looking for a finish line or planning to get to a point where we've arrived at a destination. Just as in our Christian walk we are to renew our minds consistently, so we always will be in the process of moving from blindness to sight.

I vividly recall many conversations with mentors of color in which I sheepishly asked a version of this same question: What are the mile markers that indicate I'm experiencing authentic awakenings? I was aware that what *awake* meant for me may be irrelevant to a larger set of questions that I needed to be asking. So this chapter is an overview of the seven markers that confirm that we're experiencing awakenings needed to continue moving down the path of cultural identity development.

Marker 1: Becoming Theologically Awake

Given that I'm writing this book for those who are looking at racial justice through the lens of faith, it's appropriate that we fix the first marker on a deeper revelation of the character of God. In his book *Knowledge of the Holy*, A. W. Tozer said, "What comes into our minds when we think about God is the most important thing about us."[1] I couldn't agree more with this quote. There's nothing that shapes our actions and behaviors more than how we see God.

Colossians 2:6-10 tells us that in Christ Jesus we see the full expression of the character of God. And when we surrender our lives to him as Lord, we are brought into his fullness. Therefore, an awakening to justice, reconciliation, and cultural identity begins with seeing the full expression of Jesus with increasing clarity. To be awake is to see Jesus as he identified his mission, as stated in his hometown of Nazareth when he opened the scrolls of Isaiah in the synagogue and said,

"The Spirit of the Lord is on me,
    because he has anointed me
    to proclaim good news to the poor.
He has sent me to proclaim freedom for the prisoners
    and recovery of sight for the blind,
to set the oppressed free,
    to proclaim the year of the Lord's favor. . . .
Today this scripture is fulfilled in your hearing."
(Luke 4:18-19, 21)

To know Jesus is to know the one who is anointed by the Spirit to proclaim freedom, to heal the blind, and to liberate the oppressed. This is how Jesus introduced himself, and it remained central to his identity.

When John the Baptist was imprisoned for preaching about Jesus, he was understandably shaken. His faith was wavering, and he wanted to ensure that he had indeed seen clearly. John sent some servants to confirm, and this is what Jesus told them:

When the men came to Jesus, they said, "John the Baptist sent us to you to ask, 'Are you the one who is to come, or should we expect someone else?'"

At that very time Jesus cured many who had diseases, sicknesses and evil spirits, and gave sight to many who were blind. So he replied to the messengers, "Go back and report to John what you have seen and heard: The blind receive sight, the lame walk, those who have leprosy are cleansed, the deaf hear, the dead are raised, and the good news is proclaimed to the poor." (Luke 7:20-22)

Jesus identified himself with those on the margins right up to the end. He famously used the imagery of sheep (righteous) and goats (unrighteous) to represent those who understood his ministry and those who did not:

> Then the King will say to those on his right, "Come, you who are blessed by my Father; take your inheritance, the kingdom prepared for you since the creation of the world. For I was hungry and you gave me something to eat, I was thirsty and you gave me something to drink, I was a stranger and you invited me in, I needed clothes and you clothed me, I was sick and you looked after me, I was in prison and you came to visit me." (Matthew 25:34-36)[2]

Jesus bluntly stated that the difference between those who knew him and those who didn't came down to *seeing*. After commending the righteous for seeing him in the hungry, the thirsty, the immigrant, and the naked (Matthew 25:37-40), he rebuked the unrighteous for failing to see him: "They also will answer, 'Lord, when did we see you hungry or thirsty or a stranger or needing clothes or sick or in prison, and did not help you?' He will reply, 'Truly I tell you, whatever you did not do for one of the least of these, you did not do for me'" (Matthew 25:44-45).

To be theologically awake is to take these words of Jesus seriously: "No one can see the kingdom of God unless they are born again" (John 3:3). It is also to embrace the fact that a spiritual rebirth ushers in both the salvation of our souls and our participation in the redemption of this world. It is also to hold together activism and evangelism; protest and prayer; personal piety and social justice; intimacy with Jesus and proximity to the poor.

Marker 2: Recognizing the Kingdom Battle over the Imago Dei

When Jesus said no one can see the kingdom of God unless they are born again, he was pointing to a contest between two rival kingdoms. Therefore, it follows that one of the first and most important signs of transformational awakening is a newfound ability to recognize and distinguish between these two kingdoms as well as to identify the battle line accurately.

The kingdom of God is a sweeping term encompassing every dimension of a Christian's life. But there's no need for the broad scope to distract us from what is most esteemed in God's kingdom: human beings. God has affection for us that eclipses anything else in the created order. As human beings, we're created in the image of God, are known and set apart before birth, are knit together in our mother's womb, are of such importance to the Father that he knows the individual hairs on our head, are specifically sought after by Jesus, and have an angelic party thrown in our honor whenever we repent and turn to God (Genesis 1:26; Jeremiah 1:5; Psalm 139:13; Matthew 10:30; Luke 19:10; 15:10).

This is why the sin of racism is so serious. The system of race, at its core, is a revaluation of human worth. Instead of ordering human value around the doctrine of the *imago Dei*, it ascribes value based on proximity to whiteness. Dr. Reggie Williams, a professor at McCormick Seminary, describes this historical act of playing God by ascribing value to the creation of the "white normative human being." He says that throughout American history the white male has been held up as the ideal human that everyone else is measured against. "It is what historically allowed us to colonize Native people, subject Black people to slavery, to control immigration narratives for Latino and Asian people, etc., and it still remains coded into our values."[3]

One place where we can clearly see a disturbing reordering of human value around whiteness is in portrayals of Jesus. For centuries, he has been cast as a white man in Western art, often with European features such as blue eyes and light hair. This is obviously inaccurate from a historical standpoint, yet that hasn't stopped us from accommodating that image.

I was with a white friend once at St. Sabina's Church on the South Side of Chicago, which has a large mural of a black Jesus on the ceiling. He began to grumble under his breath that it was sacrilegious to portray Jesus in a historically inaccurate way. I reminded him that not only was Jesus a Jewish, Middle Eastern man, but as a carpenter he surely spent a lot of time in the sun. If one had to guess which side of the dark/light spectrum his skin was, it would be reasonable to assume dark. I challenged this friend to take note of the unexamined ways race had shaped the way he viewed everything, in light of a black Jesus seeming sacrilegious while a white Jesus was comfortable for him. I also challenged him to research ways that portrayals of Jesus as white have impacted nonwhite minorities.

For the person whom God has awakened, recognizing the *imago Dei* is one of the preeminent battles in our country's legacy. It is, in effect, a brawl between two warring kingdoms. The kingdom of this world continues to accommodate and promote a racial hierarchy that values people based on their proximity to whiteness. It attempts to erase the story of native people, to perpetuate a narrative that says black people are dangerous, and to portray Mexican immigrants as an economic threat. It attempts either to render Asian Americans as invisible or to paint them as a monolithic group—and one that can be used as pawns against black people. All the while, it attempts to deceive white people into cowering in fear and trying to protect what we believe is our racial birthright.

The kingdom of God, on the other hand, has a completely different narrative. It shouts from the mountaintops that all human beings are created in the image of God and are therefore inherently valuable. It says that Jesus Christ has come to tear down the old visions of humanity that divide and to create in and through him "one new humanity" (Ephesians 2:15). It says that we who are in Christ are new creations, armed with the vision of reconciliation and sent into the world bearing witness to God's kingdom.

Marker 3: No Longer Being Defensive About White Supremacy

The term *white supremacy* tends to trigger defensive reactions and is often taken personally as an accusation of racism. But once you've crossed the threshold of awakening, you understand that there is a fundamental difference between the *system* of white supremacy (which must be challenged and ultimately dismantled) and the personhood of white *individuals* (who are made in the image of God and are therefore inherently worthy and valuable). The system of white supremacy is the offspring of the dark powers of this world, a descriptor used by the apostle Paul: "Finally, be strong in the Lord and in his mighty power. Put on the full armor of God, so that you can take your stand against the devil's schemes. For our struggle is not against flesh and blood, but against the rulers, against the authorities, against the powers of this dark world and against the spiritual forces of evil in the heavenly realms" (Ephesians 6:10-12).

Zora Neale Hurston, an African American novelist and short story writer, was a significant literary figure in the Harlem Renaissance, along with Langston Hughes and Wallace Thurman. In her seminal 1937 novel, *Their Eyes Were Watching God*, she wrote, "Common danger made common friends. Nothing sought a conquest over the other." The common danger (Hurston's term) that makes common friends out of all of us is the power of darkness (the apostle Paul's term). In this context, the enemy goes by the name "white supremacy." The battle should never be seen as one waged against "flesh and blood" but instead against the system of darkness that attacks those made of flesh and blood.

And that is exactly what white supremacy does. It attacks the humanity of *every* living being. It attacks the personhood of people of color by promoting a hateful view that they are subhuman (*sub* comes from the Latin "under" or "less than"). It attacks the personhood of those white people by promoting a hateful view that they/ we are *supra*human (*supra* comes from the Latin "above" or "beyond normal"). The enemy is not each other; it is the system of white supremacy and the evil one who leverages it for destructive purposes. We all need to have our humanity restored and recalibrated to what and who God says we are.

The only way we can move past defensiveness about white supremacy is to realize what it is and what it is not, a task that will be daunting during the early stages of the journey. Without being born again and starting over in a new kingdom reality, we have almost no chance of making the distinction. When we hear about white supremacy, superiority, and anything else in that lexical family, our natural reaction is to assume we're being attacked. But once we can identify it as a system, principality, and power of darkness, we realize there's nothing left to defend. In fact, we realize that our own interests are at stake, for that system dehumanizes us as much as it does anyone else.

Brandon Green, a pastor on our staff, summarizes this distinction between the danger of the system and the value of individuals in a crisp manner: "As Christians, we are trying to kill white supremacy without killing white people." To a person new to this journey, that statement may sound threatening. But to someone awakened to the kingdom reality of race in our country, it makes perfect sense.

That's why I've come to believe that a white person's reaction to the term *white supremacy* is the most tangible sign of his or her being awake or not. Once white supremacy is understood as the evil and dangerous system it is, the common enemy becomes abundantly clear. The enemy is not each other; this is not white people versus people of color. No, the enemy is white supremacy, and the evil one leverages that system for destructive purposes. It's a dark and dangerous system, and it must be opposed and dismantled at all costs.

Remember Drew Hart's story of a white woman who joined a group of Christian reconcilers for an honest discussion on race, and the contents of the discussion caused her insides to start spinning? Despite an interest in growing in this area, she felt threatened by the conversation around white supremacy to the point that she began to mishear things, such as thinking participants were saying white people can't be Christian. Hart asked her a number of follow-up questions, and I think the most important was this: Is it possible that conflicting emotions from the conversation were a sign of still drawing a substantial amount of self-worth from being white?

This was a profound yet practical question because it got to the heart of this third marker: defensiveness. He asked if she had awakened to the point that she could differentiate between the system of white supremacy, which is evil, and her innate value as a white human being, which was not being challenged. The fact that she couldn't do so was not a condemnation of her character or a devaluing of her personhood. It was simply a reality check. She was awakening but still had some distance to go before her own identity was free from being propped up by subliminal messages about whiteness.

The ability to no longer be defensive about white supremacy is a significant mark in the journey of blindness-to-sight and toward cultural identity development. It means you see the distinction between your worth and value as someone created in the image of God as well as the false set of values ascribed to you (and others) by white supremacy.

You realize that who you are in Jesus is beautiful and precious and worth living from at all costs and that the message of white supremacy is sinful and something you have to untangle yourself from.

Marker 4: Dismantling White Supremacy Trumps the Seeking of Diversity

Being confident and clear in identifying white supremacy is central to the awakening process, and I assume this as we explore the four remaining markers. One of the most immediate implications of this clear vision is that the awakened person has a new respect for what diversity can and can't do. He learns to see a lack of diversity as the branch of the tree and white supremacy as the root.

One of the first blindness-to-sight discoveries for a white person (or church) tends to be the aha moment when she realizes her world is almost entirely white. When this epiphany happens, there's an almost immediate desire to pursue diversity. For a white individual, the pursuit happens through forming friendships with people of color. For the white congregation, it happens through diverse populations merging into the congregation. The reflex to pursue immediate diversity is understandable, as it often appears to be the logical next step upon discovering the Eurocentric nature of friendships and ecclesial circles. Yet this approach is fraught with problems. When our first attempt is to pursue diversity, we risk prioritizing the secondary problem (lack of relationship) over the primary and most threatening problem (white supremacy).

Crossing the threshold of awakening reverses this order. Transformative revelation allows us to see that the lack of diversity is not and never was the result of a random set of social factors; instead it's a direct fruit of the legacy of white supremacy. We come to terms with the fact that since the time we were born we have been conditioned to prize whiteness and to associate it with all things good—beauty, intelligence, capacity, etc. We come to terms with the fact that we were steered as young people toward "good" schools districts, "good" neighborhoods, "good" universities, and "good" jobs. We didn't have the eyes to see it then, and we now realize that "good" was the politically safe way to say "white." This normalization of the goodness of whiteness has led to a lack of diverse experience, and we realize it has shaped us as white people in a very specific and unique way.

Transformational vision allows us to see that the root of all these problems is white supremacy and that the growth of its branches is the racial segregation that we now find ourselves afflicted with. This is the epiphany that most matters; it puts the problem of lack of diversity in its proper place. It also gives us clarity about how to prioritize our efforts: nothing is more critical than to pursue the dismantling of white supremacy, both in the prisons of our own minds and in the toxic structures that everyday people participate in. From there we can pursue diversity, but only when the main priority is clear.

Let me share a story that illustrates the difference between early sight and advanced sight on this front. A pastor of a large, suburban, white church asked for advice on diversifying his congregation. He shared his enthusiasm about a recent epiphany he'd had about racial justice and told me he and his board had made a commitment to add at least two nonwhite employees to the team over the next twelve months. He then asked for guidance on setting that process up.

Rather than giving him suggestions, I asked, "What do you hope will happen to the church as a result of hiring two staff people of color?" He was ready for this question and answered quickly: "I want my congregation to know that our leadership is serious about this vision. I believe that the best way for them to know how serious we are is to back it up by hiring people of color."

That sounded great, and I could see he was serious about it. I also recognized it may be the beginnings of a transformational awakening, so I continued to probe. "How will you create structures and systems for allowing these staff members to speak into any vestiges of white supremacy that they discover in the culture of your church?"

This question threw him for a loop. He hadn't thought about this angle, and to his credit, he was very transparent about that. He said, "I don't think I could use the phrase *white supremacy* within my church. They aren't ready for it yet." I thanked him for his humility and candor. I told him that if he continued to walk in spirit of truth, love, and humility, he would come to see God's kingdom in new ways.

We spent the next hour talking about the relationship between white supremacy and diversity, and he developed a new appreciation for the prioritization of each one. He began to realize that hiring staff of color might be a detrimental first step for the journey God had that church on. After all, how could he possibly empower the new staff to speak into vestiges of white supremacy if the congregants were unable even to utter the term? And how could he protect the new staff from the backlash when they began to challenge the historical assumptions of that institution? It was a nearly impossible task that would guarantee pain and sorrow. While I very much hoped he would be able to figure out how to seek diversity in the leadership team, it was also clear that a lot of shepherding needed to happen to get his white congregation ready for it.

This same dynamic applies to the awakening white person who longs to have diverse friendships. We tend to underappreciate two dynamics when we seek crosscultural interactions, and we save both our friends and ourselves a lot of pain if we take the time to consider them up front: First, we should count the cost of what we're trying to accomplish. Second, we should count the cost of what it will require of our friend.

Count the cost for yourself. If the only reason you pursue friendship with a person of color is because diversity seems to be the next step, take a lengthy pause before moving forward. The primary enemy of God's kingdom in this realm is white supremacy, and what we need in our transformational journey is friends who can help us understand what that means. So if the purpose of a friendship is to learn to see and dismantle white supremacy, that's a great reason to pursue friendship. But even then, you must be ready for the challenge this will pose to your upbringing and views. If you're feeling sensitive about probing around the idea of white supremacy, it's not fair to pursue your future friend without letting that person know where you stand. Pursue your own awakening journey outside the context of crosscultural friendships until you truly long for that type of interaction.

Count the cost for your friend. If you're white, and you're pursuing friendships with people of color who can help you understand white supremacy, take into account what it may cost them. In a conversation in which I was talking about my illumination about race with an African American friend, her eyes suddenly welled with tears. When I asked her what was wrong, she said that though she valued conversations and though she was glad for my progress, such conversations were often very painful for her. She said, "I believe that the gospel calls me to participate in the journey of enlightenment in friends like you, and I'm happy to do so. But the truth is that every traumatic memory I've experienced is associated with race, and every time I talk about those, it's as if I'm reliving the trauma. There's a human part of me that wonders why I put myself through this time and time again."

A number of friends of color read the draft of this book, and almost all of them double-underlined this point. We must be conscientious about the cost that comes for our friends of color when we ask them to play this role.

Everything I've explored under this marker to this point assumes that the white person is taking the initiative. But what happens when the one taking the initiative is a person of color? What if he's the one that challenges you to become more aware of the presence of white supremacy?

The percentages show that they are far more likely to be initiators, and that brings the truth of this marker into sharp focus. If we're unable to realize the presence of white supremacy, we aren't going to be able to listen to the wisdom being offered to us. And if diversity becomes the limit of what we desire, our cultural identity journey will stall. Holy Spirit awakenings must translate into an ability to challenge the ideology of white supremacy.

Marker 5: Changing the Evaluation of Growth from "What Am I Supposed to Do?" to "How Well Do I See?"

I have frequently made reference to the tendency of white people to ask the question "What am I supposed to do?" when embarking on a quest to understand cultural identity. Nikki Toyama-Szeto, a brilliant thinker on race and justice, confirms that this reflex is one of the most important dynamics to address when attempting to progress down the road of enlightenment. Nikki is a vice president within the International Justice Mission, and her role includes directing the IJM Institute for Biblical

Justice. She has trained thousands of white people across North America and beyond, and she believes that the tendency to start the exploration journey here is a direct reflection of WASP (white, Anglo-Saxon Protestant) influence on our culture.[4] This acronym is a broad (and some would say insufficient) label that describes an aggregate of high-status and influential white Americans of English Protestant ancestry that played an instrumental role in establishing American values well into the twentieth century.

White Protestantism would eventually split into two mutually hostile camps—liberals and fundamentalists—that had controlled a disproportionate percentage of the financial, political, and social power in the United States until then. While there are many defining marks associated with the influence of WASP culture on America today, what directly applies to this fourth sign is the way they tended to approach problem solving, according to Toyama-Szeto. Those shaped by the Protestant culture often feel we need to dissect something to understand it; we need to take it apart and put it back together again before it makes sense to us. This drive is what motivates many of us to ask, "What am I supposed to do?" as a starting point and to feel frustrated when we don't get a clear answer.

We do this instinctively partly because we're looking for concrete ways to move forward, and that question highlights something worth affirming. But this sits upon a highly dangerous assumption, and that is the part of the question that begs to be seen with greater clarity. When we allow our cultural ethos to shape how we approach problems of racial justice, we easily miss the greatest problem of all: our conditioned blindness. We aren't engineers who need technical training on how to disassemble and reassemble the pieces of race; instead, we are blind wanderers who need help to see a world that functions according to a different set of rules than what we've been raised with. Said another way, we aren't Nicodemuses who need just a little push over the edge; we must be reborn through the power of Jesus in order to see his kingdom.

Embracing blindness-to-sight as our primary transformational motif has many important benefits. It helps us know how to engage with our friends of color in a new way. It helps us to avoid self-righteousness, because no one ever graduates into the position of authoritative expert. Embracing blindness-to-sight keeps us hungry and humble. Embracing blindness-to-sight helps us to remember that while sincerity and good intentions matter, they aren't to be confused with a genuine transformation of our vision.

In chapter six, I opened with the healing of the blind man in Mark 8. After Jesus spit into the blind man's eyes, he asked, "Do you see anything?" When preaching on this passage, Dr. Timothy Keller used humor to underscore the importance of being honest about the progression of sight, saying, "If the man had never admitted that he could not see right, maybe Jesus would not have finished healing him. What if after Jesus asked him if he could see right the man answered, 'Yes, I see fine.' That man would have then spent the rest of his life cutting down people and talking to trunks."[5]

I love this as a metaphor for the cultural identity journey. Moving from blindness to sight is a process, and it's imperative that we maintain a grasp on it being a central part of our transformational work. When "What am I supposed to do?" trumps "How do I learn to see?" the result is often the equivalent of cutting down people and talking to trees. The white person who has crossed the threshold of awakening never loses sight of the most important question of all: "How well do I see?"

Marker 6: Recognizing Privilege Faster and with Greater Precision

Another major mile marker of awakening is an increased comfort with acknowledging the reality of privilege. This is a natural extension of awakening to white supremacy. In the same way challenges to this system aren't meant to be emotional attacks at a personal level, conversations around the special rights or advantages granted as a result of privilege are independent of a white person's value or identity. The awakened white person therefore realizes that blindness-to-sight applies to privilege as well as supremacy, and she is on the lookout for two different manifestations of privilege blindness.

The first step in overcoming privilege blindness is recognizing that it exists; we get faster and more precise at seeing its everyday manifestations. For example, when I walk down a street in my neighborhood, I recognize that none of my neighbors cross the street to avoid passing me or lock their doors as a safety precaution against me. But that's not the experience of residents of color, who are often perceived as unsafe. When a police officer drives down the street in my neighborhood looking for potential problems, they look right past me. Yet when they spot a young black or brown person, the chances are high that they'll stop and interrogate that person. I've witnessed this firsthand dozens of times and watched as a random frisk escalated into a problematic situation. It's heartbreaking that I'm immediately screened out as a potential threat, due to my privilege, while innocent youths experience the opposite. These examples scratch the surface of everyday manifestations of privilege that we can now recognize faster and with greater precision.

A second form of privilege blindness is recognizing our own privilege yet remaining blind to the ways privilege continues to blind us. We must grasp that while our social status privileges us in certain ways, it handicaps us in others. There are literally whole dimensions of reality we don't understand because of privilege, and certain lenses through which we've learned to view the world must be challenged fundamentally. Though it's significant to be able to overcome the first form of privilege blindness (recognizing it exists), it's important that we not treat it as a box we check and then move on to life as usual without having checks and balances that help us to continue the awakening process.

Too often I've seen white people discover that they have privilege but then treat that recognition as an all-access pass to push forward into their personal agenda for solving problems without any checks or balances on their privilege. While it's an important step to become aware of one's privilege, the impact of that awareness becomes diffused if we don't put steps in place to monitor and challenge that privilege.

The most effective way to guard against this tendency is to make a personal commitment to never lead from privilege without first accessing the voices of those on the margins—particularly those most affected by whatever endeavor you're undertaking. A great biblical case study for this is Acts 6. In a spirit of caring for the vulnerable, the apostles instituted a food-sharing program for the widows of the community. It served widows of two different cultural backgrounds that were having very different experiences with the food giveaway. The first group of widows was of Hebrew origin, and as such had direct access to the dominant culture of the time. The second group was of Grecian origin, and they felt that their outsider status was resulting in their marginalization when the food was distributed.

This is an important story in the New Testament because it's the first time we see a conflict involving power and privilege in the emerging church. Luke is the author of the book of Acts, and as a Gentile outsider, he seemed to be curious to see how the early church would respond. Would the apostles recognize the dynamics of power and privilege, or would they dismiss the complaints?

Presumably Luke was delighted as the situation was handled delicately and thoughtfully. Rather than exercising their privilege and making a unilateral decision on behalf of those who were being marginalized, the apostles first paid significant attention to those who were experiencing pain. They empowered the group most affected by the problem to solve their own problem and created a pathway for leaders in the marginalized group to emerge. It was both effective and honoring of everyone in the community. This is a model for racial awakening: we see that we have privilege and that analyzing that privilege must be a communal affair.

Marker 7: Living in a State of Hopeful Lament

This final marker comes in the form of a two-part phrase: hopeful lament. When I reflect on the lament side of the phrase, I'm reminded of the sobering words of one of the twentieth century's greatest writers and social critics, James Baldwin: "To be a Negro in this country and to be relatively conscious is to be in a rage almost all the time." While I'll never know even a modicum of what it's like to be black in America, I imagine that the heart of his statement could extend to all residents of this country.

When we become even relatively awake—or to use Baldwin's term, conscious—we begin to see with increasing clarity the ways our system of race has dehumanized everyone as well as led to suffering for many on the margins. There's no way to be conscious of this without feeling grief. I have come to believe we aren't supposed to ignore, anesthetize, or screen out this grief. In fact, if I can be audacious enough, I will suggest a corollary quote, but for white people: "To be a white person in this country and to be relatively conscious is to be in a state of lament almost all the time." To be awake is to see clearly the sorrows that come in this world.

Lament is a beautiful and needed resource because it has a unique way of remaining awake to sorrow without succumbing to it. Lament allows us to grieve injustice but not fall into despair. We can be awake to the pain of the world but still press forward in faith because of another beautiful word at the center of the gospel: *hope.*

In an interview with *Frontline*, Harvard professor Dr. Cornel West, another modern-day freedom fighter, was asked if he was optimistic about where America is heading. Here is how he answered:

I am not optimistic, but I've never been optimistic about humankind or America. The evidence never looks good in terms of forces for good actually becoming prominent. But I am a prisoner of hope, and that's very different. I believe that we do have signs of hope, and that the evidence is underdetermined. We have to make a leap of faith beyond the evidence and try to energize one another so we can accent the best in one another. But that is what being a prisoner of hope is all about.[6]

I have found this to be a helpful way to describe the state of an awakened Christ-follower. *Optimism* rarely feels like the right word. When dominant-culture folks try to portray our national progress in optimistic terms, they sound tone-deaf to the struggles of so many on the margins. But West says that doesn't stop him from being a "prisoner of hope," a term lifted directly from Zechariah 9:12.

To be awake is to lament that much is wrong with the world, but to be awake also means we are prisoners of hope. We remember that hope was never found in our ideas, solutions, or proposals in the first place; hope always has been and always will be found in Christ alone. We remember that Jesus will eventually make all things right and that our hope is found in this truth. But we remember that he is ushering in the kingdom of God—right here and right now. We are to pray for God's kingdom to come on earth as it is in heaven, right here and right now. We are to believe in his power and his redemption. We are to remain prisoners of hope!

While we'll always need to humbly seek revelation, knowledge, wisdom, and insight, we also affirm mile markers of awakening along the way. These signposts point to the activity of the Spirit of God in our lives and continue to drive us forward in seeking first God's kingdom.

Active Participation

"What am I supposed to do?"

I have referred to this question at multiple points throughout this book and have explored why it can be dangerous if asked in isolation of the transformational blindness-to-sight journey. Left unexamined, this question suggests that moving into problem-solving mode is the logical and expedient step in the process for white people, and it simultaneously discounts the major handicap that our blindness to racial patterns, systems, and structures brings to the equations. It's my deep conviction that the primary work of Jesus in our lives is to rescue us from the shadows of this current kingdom and lead us to the light as he brings into view the kingdom of God.

With that being said, I don't want to minimize the role of concrete action. Christ's life tended to follow the pattern of contemplation (that is, seeing) and then action (that is, doing), and the realm of cultural identity is no different. Once we see differently, we should indeed act differently, and that pattern should be evident at regular junctures of our cultural identity journey. This chapter proposes some action steps that can be paired with the stages of awakening.

One last disclaimer before jumping in: I'm not certain what term to use to describe this last stage. The term *white ally* is the most commonly used for those who align with the interests of people of color, but that term has begun to fall out of favor. Some use the term *accomplice* as a replacement, but that hasn't achieved mainstream acceptance. So I've chosen to use the term *active participant*, as it seems in line with the spirit of the command of Jesus to "seek the Kingdom of God above all else, and live righteously" (Matthew 6:33 NLT).

With that, here are some important actions steps that can accompany the different stages of the awakening journey.

Continue to Educate Yourself

It's important that we each take responsibility for continuing the journey of educating ourselves, and there are a variety of ways we can be deliberate about that. A first and easy step is to subscribe to the work of my friend, Latasha Morrison, who created an online community called Be the Bridge to Racial Unity.[1] There are now thousands of members who regularly learn from a variety of practitioners, theologians, and academics. You'll find a steady stream of helpful resources there that will stimulate your learning about cultural identity.

Also be intentional and diligent about reading and listening to voices you might not typically align with ideologically. There's a consistent temptation to carry preexisting views shaped by political and theological leanings (that is, left/right, liberal/conservative) into explorations of cultural identity and racial awareness. While there's nothing wrong with having defined viewpoints and inner convictions, be mindful that few things shape our biases more than social location. When we don't allow our viewpoints to be challenged by those on different points of the ideological spectrum, we miss the chance to sharpen our critical-thinking skills and to unearth blind spots. Such lack of engagement can place unnecessary restrictions on developing a holistic, 360-degree kingdom perspective.

Let me share an example from my journey of engaging with multiple viewpoints. One of the social issues that became paramount for me in my racial awakening was that of poverty—particularly poverty affecting children. Dietrich Bonhoeffer, a World War II–era pastor, theologian, and activist, said, "The ultimate test of a society's morality is how it treats its children." In America, the richest nation on earth, one in five children lives in poverty. This means one out of every five of our children is in constant danger of harm, because statistics show that poverty drastically reduces the possibility of a child getting a good education and having access to health care, while also increasing their chances of entering prison. When you add race to that equation, the danger level skyrockets. This is what led Dr. Marian Wright Edelman, one of my heroes, to claim, "The most dangerous place for a child to grow up today is at the intersection of race and poverty."[2]

Once this became clear to me, I knew I could no longer live in middle-class environments sheltered from the plight of those navigating poverty. So I followed some of the suggestions that you'll see later in this chapter: I made a lifetime commitment to stay proximate to suffering, and I consistently served with organizations that worked with families in poverty. But what about this first point? How would I continue to educate myself? How would I best expose myself to new areas of thought and be mindful to engage with those whose views were different from mine?

I began to discover that within the realm of scholarship on poverty is a sharp ideological split over solutions. Those on the more conservative side argue that the solution involves personal responsibility: nurturing the family unit, teaching life skills, instilling morals, and so on. Those on the more liberal side argue that the solution falls more on the side of social justice: addressing root causes such as housing discrimination, failing schools, and the lack of economic opportunity in low-income neighborhoods. I had my own beliefs and biases that nudged me in a certain direction, but I also realized that my social location and personal experience had played a large role in forming that bias. Therefore I made a commitment to educate myself on the best thinking and practices from both sides of the ideological divide.

One of the most concrete and enriching learning experiences that helped facilitate my continuing education was a book club that intentionally studied two competing philosophies. The first book was *Bridges Out of Poverty* by Dr. Ruby Payne, who is arguably the most visible educator about poverty and who provides materials and workshops for teachers and administrators across the country. Payne's approach revolves around personal responsibility; she believes that if children in poverty are going to prosper, they need to develop a specific set of skills. Included in this proposed skill set is building and keeping relationships, getting one's needs met, communicating in middle-class vernacular, and entertaining and being entertained. Payne asserts that children growing up in a culture of poverty don't succeed because they have been taught the "hidden rules of poverty" so they are unaware of the hidden rules of the middle class.

The second book we read was *An African Centered Response to Ruby Payne's Poverty Theory* by Dr. Jawanza Kunjufu, a well-respected Afrocentric educator and the author of more than sixty-five books. He took exception to what is often called the "blame the victim" approach to alleviating poverty: the onus falls on those victimized by the system to find a way to pull themselves up by the bootstraps. He felt that Payne located the problem of poverty with the people born into the system rather than engaging in a critical analysis of why those systems exist in the first place. He rebuked her use of deficit theory (poor people are poor because of their own deficiencies) and took exception to her belief that success for poor children is defined in relationship to their ability to live a middle-class lifestyle. He then laid out his own vision for addressing poverty, focusing on the rebuilding of vital systems on a neighborhood-by-neighborhood basis.

The members of the book club fell on different points of the left/right, personal responsibility/systemic justice spectrums, and therefore were challenged by the conflicting convictions in each of the books. Engaging in honest exploration of each voice resulted in a rich and dynamic atmosphere, and we walked away feeling wiser and more seasoned. So I recommend studying with people with different philosophies. There is no one voice that can help you engage cultural identity, so it's wise to educate yourself by listening to a wide spectrum of voices.

Get Proximate to Suffering

In chapter four, "Encounter," I shared a quote from Bryan Stevenson, the founder of the Equal Justice Initiative. Stevenson is regularly called on to speak on the concrete steps that white people can take when responding to our growing awakening. His advice always begins with the same call to action: get proximate to suffering. He argues that this is the core gospel message ("to me, the Great Commission is a call to get approximate"[3]) and that this pattern is evident in the life of Jesus himself.

One of his most succinct descriptions of getting proximate was in a graduation speech at Wesleyan University's 2016 commencement ceremony:

The first thing I believe you have to do is that you have to commit to getting proximate to the places in our nation, in our world, where there's suffering and abuse and neglect. Many of you have been taught your whole lives that there are parts of the community where the schools don't work very well; if there are sections of the community where there's a lot of violence or abuse or despair or neglect, you should stay as far away from those parts of town as possible. Today, I want to urge you to do the opposite. I think you need to get closer to the parts of the communities where you live where there's suffering and abuse and neglect. I want you to choose to get closer. We have people trying to solve problems from a distance, and their solutions don't work, because until you get close, you don't understand the nuances and the details of those problems. And I am persuaded that there is actually power in proximity.[4]

We must remain aware of the temptation to educate ourselves from an ivory tower. I'm a strong advocate of reading books, listening to podcasts, watching TED talks, and engaging with any other form of intellectual education, but I'm also conscious of the limits these place on our ability to be fully awake. Our history of race has resulted in a variety of inequalities throughout society, and we can't fully understand these inequalities from a distance. We can learn about ideas like race, culture, and identity in a classroom setting, but it's far more transformational to learn through actual proximity to suffering.

I often speak with white people who resonate with this point but are unable to imagine how to move from their comfortable quarters into greater proximity with suffering. There are certainly no one-size-fits-all answers to this question. In his book *Irresistible Revolution*, my friend Shane Claiborne tells the story of a summer that he spent with Mother Teresa. That ten-week period had a profound impact on his development, but it left him uncertain about how he could continue the work when he returned to Philadelphia. Feeling desperate, he asked Mother Teresa for advice. She replied, "Calcuttas are everywhere if only we have eyes to see. Find your Calcutta."[5]

It should come as no surprise that at the center of these wise words is a call to increased awakening. Mother Teresa was reminding Shane that the problem wasn't just the absence of suffering in his hometown; it was his inability to *see* the suffering. When we pray to have our eyes opened, as Mother Teresa urged Shane to do, God transforms our vision in unexpected ways. We can never discount the role of the Holy Spirit as we look for ways to become more proximate to the suffering all around us.

Explore Ways to Share Your Social Network

One leader that has really shaped my thinking around the concrete action that white people can take is Pastor Dee McIntosh, founder of the Lighthouse Covenant Church in Minneapolis.[6] She says that one of her biblical heroes is Nehemiah, whose reconciliation story reflects a number of justice-savvy qualities that should be emulated as we embark on our own journey. She points out that this Old Testament account opens with a grim report on the city of Jerusalem, which had been laid to waste by the Babylonians and then by the Assyrians.

All the able-bodied Jewish men, women, and children were captive, so the only inhabitants left were orphans and widows. The city no longer had the means and resources to accommodate the needs of the people, nor could it protect them from the destructive forces that intended to harm them. The urban Jews were displaced, dispossessed, and disenfranchised. Hanani, one of Nehemiah's brothers, headed to the palace to share the "great trouble and disgrace" of the residents (Nehemiah 1:3).

In the best sermon I've ever heard on the book of Nehemiah, Pastor Dee named four traits that Nehemiah demonstrated when he heard of the pain in the city: First, he took seriously the report from the people who were in the midst of the suffering, and he didn't insist on confirmation from outside sources to validate the reality of the misery. Second, he responded by entering into an extended period of lament. Third, he repented—first for ancestral sin, second for the sins of the Israelite nation, third for his own complicity. Fourth, and finally, he responded with concrete action (Nehemiah 1:2, 4, 6-10, 11).[7]

Each of the first three steps was of critical importance and was covered in previous chapters. The fourth step is the most germane to this chapter, and Pastor Dee described Nehemiah's concrete response like this:

> Nehemiah recognizes the context in which he lives. He recognizes that he is in a seat of privilege that those in the inner city

do not have. He recognizes that he has the capacity to influence people who look just like him, who come from the same context as him, and have resources, and he takes all of those resources that he has into the inner city of Jerusalem and he says, "How might I work with you?"[8]

She then expanded on the resources he had and focused on the social capital of Nehemiah as a high-ranking member of the king's court. When he was awakened to the pain of the city, he took the risk to access and then spend that social capital and to share those resources with the people who most desperately needed them.

Nehemiah recognized many important things, but let's focus on just one integrated idea: becoming aware of our social capital and networks and then spending that capital for the cause of reconciliation and justice. Here are two questions we can regularly ask ourselves:

◆ What social capital do I have access to?

◆ In what ways can I spend that social capital for the sake of justice?

I've tried to ask these questions of myself at each stage of my development, and the answers have evolved during the various seasons of my life. For example, when I left the Willow Creek staff, I had one kind of social capital to spend. I wasn't aware of that capital at the time, but leaving to plant a church in the city was celebrated widely by a number of white, suburban churches. This was bizarre to me, as I didn't see what I was doing as particularly noble, and I expected to fail. But my insecurities did nothing to stop a strange narrative from forming that made me seem like a heroic figure: "Young white pastor leaves comfort of the riches of Willow Creek and goes to plant a church among the poor of the inner city."

This was not a narrative I started, and I did everything I could to curtail it, but I was aware of its persistence. It made me sad, because it was one more reminder of how disconnected the white church is from churches led by people of color. There were amazing, persistent, rooted, trustworthy ministries doing important work, but for all kinds of reasons they were (and are) ignored by most of the white church. And when a privileged, educated person like me leaves the comforts of white Christianity to join in this work, we talk about it in almost messianic ways.

Much more could be said about this dynamic, but that would take me too far off the point. Despite the obvious flaws in this preferential treatment, it would have been ignorant of me to overlook the privilege that came with it and not reflect on how that privilege and social capital could be spent on behalf of justice. Using the two questions above, I reflected on how to do this best. If I put it in a Q&A format, it would have sounded like this:

Q: What social capital do I have access to?

A: The attention of dominant culture congregations who want to talk about urban church planting

Q: In what ways can I spend that social capital for the sake of justice?

A: Take myself out of the center and point their interest at churches that have been doing the work credibly for a long time

The fascination with River City's launch lasted only a year or so, but during that time I received a handful of invitations to speak about the journey of urban church planting. With the Nehemiah template in my head, I prayed and tried to find ways to recenter their interest. And I consistently declined speaking opportunities, encouraging white churches to invite pastors that had served in the city for a long time.

Over time, that form of social capital disappeared, and I had to be on the lookout for new forms of currency that could be brought to the common table. Recently, the Nehemiah principle has played out in the fundraising we do for our nonprofit arm, the River City Community

Development Center.[9] While we are like most nonprofits in that we typically feel overworked and underresourced, we understand that we are extremely privileged. While we don't have many in the River City congregation that have excess monetary wealth, we have a number that are connected to a robust social network. This has translated into our community development efforts getting far more exposure than the typical neighborhood nonprofit, and we see that as a privilege. We have therefore committed ourselves to be <u>advocates</u> for some of the other wonderful nonprofit organizations we're in relationship with and to look for ways to share our funders with their ministries as well.

No two stories are alike, so the ways you become aware of, access, and spend social capital for the sake of justice will look different from mine. But there should be lots of similar themes in our stories. We can each learn from and emulate the story of Nehemiah and follow the pattern of his efforts: hear the pain, lament the pain, repent for complicity, and join in the efforts.

Find a Place to Serve Consistently

One of the most effective ways to be transformed out of a fix-it mode and into a learn-to-see mode is to find a place where you can serve consistently. I was fortunate to receive this advice during my awakening era while working at Willow Creek, and it led me to a wonderful organization called Bethel New Life located in the West Garfield Park neighborhood of Chicago. Bethel New Life works with families that are trying to break the cycle of poverty. Each Saturday Bethel would host a series of activities and programs for the families in the neighborhood. These programs depended on volunteers, and since I was a twentysomething volunteer with a lot of free time, it was a perfect match.

I began going to Bethel two Saturdays a month, and though I enjoyed the volunteer aspect of it, I also found it to be more uncomfortable than I'd expected. For one, I realized that I was still carrying all kinds of ignorant and uninformed perspectives about those who live in poverty. I'm embarrassed to admit it, but I had been significantly shaped by the deficit theory (a term that I was unfamiliar with at the time but which is the most accurate way to classify my perspective). Again, deficit theory views poor people through a deficit lens: namely, they are poor because of their own moral and intellectual deficiencies.[10]

The version of this that I had been groomed to believe was that the fundamental problem of those living in poverty was that they didn't work hard enough. If they would develop a stronger work ethic, the narrative went, it would almost single-handedly lift them out of poverty. But as I was with these families at Bethel each Saturday, that viewpoint was challenged in a major way. What I saw were families whose work ethic put mine to shame, with many of the mothers working as many as three jobs to make ends meet. It was very uncomfortable to have my inadequate perspectives challenged in such a mighty way, and it was transformational. The ugliness of poverty disturbed me, and I haven't been the same since. I was also humbled by the grace and resilience these families showed as they navigated poverty continually, and they taught me epic lessons about faith.

The other significant lesson during that era confronted my pride. Though I had signed up with the intention of serving however Bethel needed me to volunteer, I had an unstated assumption that before long I'd take on a leadership role. After all, I was a staff worker from Willow Creek, and church leaders from around the country came to learn from our church. I didn't complain the first few times I was assigned tasks that seemed menial to me, such as overseeing craft tables and serving hot dogs. But when it became clear that these kinds of tasks might be my permanent assignment, I began to get restless. I even began to wonder if it was bad stewardship for me to have my leadership gifts underutilized, given that I was spending so much time there.

It took longer than it should have for me to find the cure to this dilemma. I eventually realized how many different forms of pride my attitude represented. I was not only overstating my own abilities, I was also understating the abilities of the men and women who ran Bethel New Life. Over time it became clear to me that those on the frontlines were the experts on what needed to happen—not me. After all, what did I even know about working with families facing abject poverty? It was ridiculous that I was feeling tension about my leadership being underutilized, though it was also predictable. This continues to be one of the classic combinations that come with early stages in the blindness-to-sight journey: an underestimation of how serious the problem is and an overestimation of our ability to effectively solve the problem.

I tell this story to emphasize the point that we need not only to find a place where we can serve consistently but also to do so without expecting to lead or be in charge. People eagerly volunteer and, in an attempt to be helpful, try to employ their ideas. We need a different posture in our service—one of waiting to be invited in. An elder at River City who coaches young leaders in our congregation says, "You may have gifts that can be shared in this environment, but wait for them to ask you for them. It's always better to be invited than to invite yourself." We'd do well to listen.

This is consistent with the posture of Jesus himself, who reminded his disciples that "the Son of Man did not come to be served, but to serve" (Mark 10:45). The path of wisdom chooses humility over pride and service over ego. When we serve consistently and humbly, it positions us to see new things and build trust with the organization. This creates a unique opportunity to go deeper in our cultural identity journey.

Place Yourself Under the Leadership of People of Color

In chapter one, I shared an exercise in which I was instructed to take an inventory of the voices that were informing me as a person. I organized the exercise around four groups of voices: my closest friends, the mentors I looked to for guidance, the preachers/teachers/theologians I relied on for spiritual guidance, and the authors of the books

I was reading. This led to the painful realization that my world had been and was continuing to be shaped almost exclusively by white voices. I knew I needed to put myself in positions where I was under the leadership of people of color.

Chances are high that, if you're white, your results would be the same. The pastors of your church, the Sunday school teachers, the mentors who speak words of life to you, your small group leader, anyone else who is a major influence for you—it's likely that this group is overwhelmingly white. It's the unavoidable fruit of living segregated lives.

The big question is, will you have the *will* to change that? I use the word *will* because placing yourself under the leadership of people of color is more difficult than it sounds. Most of us have no idea how strongly we prefer white styles of leadership, communication, decision making, etc., until we submit to a leader of color. In that new arena, we discover how life in America is lived on two different sides of a racial divide. When you're a person of color, it doesn't matter if you prefer to be under a leader from your own cultural group; you still have to learn to adapt to white leaders. But when you're white, you can choose to stay under the leadership of white people your entire life. And when you experiment with putting yourself under a leader of color, you have the choice to opt out as soon as it becomes uncomfortable for you.

Therefore, putting yourself under the leadership of a person of color is a matter of will. To do it, you must possess the will to endure if it gets uncomfortable for you. You must possess the will to check your own privilege when it flares up—which it will. You must possess the will to push forward, even when everything in you wants to give up.

Invest in White People

In chapter eight, I explored the concept of self-righteousness and the tendency we have to rest our identity on the idea of racism reflecting binary categories of good people and bad people. Rather than seeing growth as progress on a spectrum from blindness to sight, we face a constant temptation to establish a cultural identity through association with the good people and condemnation of the bad ones.

One of the casualties of an allegiance to the good/bad binary is what Dr. Robin DiAngelo refers to as "the very unhelpful phenomenon of un-friending on Facebook,"[11] where we distance ourselves from white people who don't align with our values. Because we don't want to be implicated in their badness, we literally or metaphorically excommunicate them from our friendship circle. We may believe that this shows solidarity with people of color, and we hope that the dramatic gesture confirms that we're staying awake.

Unfortunately, this type of thinking is backward. It's not a dramatic gesture at all, because one of the easiest actions we can take is to turn our back on someone who doesn't agree with us. And the tendency to engage in un-friending is one of the primary fuel sources of self-righteousness, as it promotes the false good/bad binary. Finally, it exonerates us from one of the important duties of a white-awake person: investing in other white people. DiAngelo asked, "If we don't work with each other, if we give in to that pull to separate, who have we left to deal with the white person that we've given up on and won't address?"[12]

I admit that I've fallen into this trap many times myself. It's frustrating and emotionally depleting to plead with white friends, family members, and associates to take racism seriously, and when they don't, it's easy to go to a self-righteous place and tune them out. But when this happens, everyone loses. I lose. The person I've tuned out or un-friended loses. And people of color lose, since we fail to be genuine allies in this work.

So one of the most positive, actionable things we can do to advance the cause is to resist the temptation to un-friend those that frustrate us (in whatever form we do that) and choose to invest actively in white people. This is making the choice to engage the coworker who makes a crude comment about someone of another race—not by showing him up but by taking an opportunity to talk about the history of racism. This is making the choice to engage with that uncle at the Thanksgiving table; instead of rolling your eyes when he makes a snide remark, start a discussion about how the family has dealt with (or not dealt with) race.

It may not seem like the most enticing work, but engaging with the white people in our extended community is one of the most concrete ways to make a difference. The apathy, indifference, and even hatred in the white community are the chief threats to racial progress in our country, and any little spark we can ignite is positive for the movement as a whole.

Learn to Locate Yourself

Dr. Christena Cleveland is a social psychologist, public theologian, author, and the first Associate Professor of the Practice of Reconciliation at Duke University's Divinity School. Her book *Disunity in Christ* is one of my favorite resources for racial reconciliation, especially because of the unique way she integrates social psychology and theology. In a lecture at Fuller Seminary, Cleveland introduced the term *sociological imagination*, which she defined as being able to see the social structures around us: the factors that influence who we are as individuals, the social groups and belief systems we are a part of, and how these affect us as well as the larger society.[13] In short, sociological imagination involves knowing where we're socially located in our society.

When reflecting on this notion of sociological imagination for seminarians (though it can be as easily be applied to a number of different spheres), Cleveland said, "When you go and join a church staff, or you go and join a nonprofit staff, are you taking this sociological imagination with you such that when you join this new organization, are you thinking, 'Okay, well where am I located . . . not just in the larger society, but in the context of this organization?'"[14] She then went on to ask these questions:

- ◆ Am I a majority member?
- ◆ Do people automatically think that my perspective is valuable because of the color of my skin? [15]
- ◆ Do people automatically think that my perspective is valuable because of the degree I have on my résumé?
- ◆ What does it mean for me to make things right in this context?
- ◆ Does it mean that I need to advocate more for the other people who are marginalized in this context?
- ◆ Or does it mean that I need to find out why other people are not in this context?
- ◆ Why is everyone on this committee the same race? Or why is everyone on this church staff male?

Being able to locate yourself socially may not sound complicated, but my experience suggests it's difficult for white people, especially when we are in crosscultural settings. Sometimes I think this is due to embarrassment about being white. Sometimes I think it's due to sheer unawareness. Sometimes I think it's because we want to project a spirit of cultural confidence, and we think that downplaying our whiteness will help. Whatever the reason, the result is that we have anemic sociological imaginations with a corresponding inability to self-identity our social location with clarity.

It often strikes white people as counterintuitive, but one of the best ways to develop trust and credibility in crosscultural circles is to locate yourself humbly. In my early stages of grappling with my whiteness, I frequently made the mistake of downplaying my whiteness. I hoped that if I pretended it wasn't there, it wouldn't harm anyone. But this backfired, as it placed doubt in the minds of the people of color as to whether they could trust my leadership. How could they entrust the needs that came with life in their social location to a leader who couldn't articulate the dynamics that came with his social location?

So I began to get braver with acknowledging my social location. Each time I shared in a crosscultural setting, I located myself and fully acknowledged the uncertainty I felt being in that circle as a white man. I also pledged to do my best to listen and learn humbly. This was always more vulnerable than I wanted to be, and it flew in the face of how I had been taught to view leadership. (Leaders should be confident and clear on where they're going, right?) To my surprise, this consistently engendered deeper trust and confidence among the people I was working with. They weren't looking to partner with a white leader who was unaware of his social location or unwilling to acknowledge it; they were looking for someone who could authentically and honestly ask questions about what that meant and how it affected me, them, and the world around us.

Become a Change Agent Within Your Sphere of Influence

I also like Cleveland's term *sociological imagination* because it has the potential to transform the way you interact with every social sphere you occupy: your family, your friends, your church, your school, and your work. Seeing the kingdom of God and the kingdom of this world with greater clarity positions you to recognize the ways that the battle plays out in each of those spheres and to seek ways that you can become a change agent in them. Watching this happen has been one of the unexpected joys of emphasizing cultural identity so much at River City.

Rob, who works in commercial real estate in Chicago, has been on a steady transformational journey regarding white cultural identity for the past decade, and he recently emerged as a major change agent in his industry. As his social awareness and then his sociological imagination strengthened, he began to notice not only that the commercial real estate industry was almost entirely white but also that it seemed to be systemically inaccessible to people of color. As he probed into the reasons for that, he concluded that it was largely due to the fact that most real estate jobs were obtained through friends of family or fraternity brothers already in the industry. For minorities to get into the business, they would almost have to be sought out by someone in the industry who valued diversity strongly enough to buck the trend. While that could happen in theory, Rob saw little evidence to confirm that it did.

So he began to work for greater awareness and increased justice. As someone well respected within the industry, he risks his social capital to do this. He has been talking about it at conferences, bringing it up in meetings, and consistently pushing it with leaders in the industry—and he believes his efforts are making a major impact. It started with widespread discomfort, as nobody likes having a veil of systemic racism pulled back. But the discomfort led to constructive conversations, and fruit is starting to be borne from those conversations.

Most notably Rob has partnered with the founder of a large development company to create an organization that brings awareness of the commercial real estate industry to communities that might not know much about the profession. They will team with colleges and companies to teach and train minority students in the commercial real estate industry. The organization has already garnered support from the CEOs of some of the largest companies. I suspect even more changes are to come, and it's directly tied to Rob developing a sociological imagination and combining it with the courage to do something.

I realize Rob has enough access to his industry to create change, but I believe the principles apply no matter what level of influence you have within your workplace. Some awakened individuals have had significant impacts in workplaces. Rebecca works for a national nonprofit that does great work for a marginalized people group but has a workforce that's 98 percent white. By simply having the courage to mention this racial disparity to her boss, this became a serious issue in the organization. She was asked to write a memo on the importance of being an organization that dealt with issues of marginalization both internally and externally, and that memo traveled all the way up to the CEO.

Mark works at a school in the Chicago Public Schools system, which has different standards for white students and students of color. As he has become awakened, he has used sociological imagination and courageously started a diversity committee at his school to address biases. Who knows how that might impact future directions there?

Taken together, these stories inspire us to locate ourselves, develop a sociological imagination, and then step forward courageously. We can each play an important role in instigating systemic change.

Find Some Young People to Build With

I'm a big fan of mentorship; I believe it's important that we both honor and learn life lessons from those who have walked the road longer and farther than we have. However, I think it's a mistake to fall into the trap of thinking that the only people who can or should mentor us are older and/or more experienced. Often the greatest subject matter experts on race, justice, and identity are the young people who navigate this world on a daily basis—particularly those who are coming of age in dangerous and challenging social settings.

This simple truth has revolutionized the way we think about mentorship at River City. We have a fundamental conviction that investing in the young people of our community is the most important kingdom work we can do, and for a long time we've been encouraging adults to get involved at our church by mentoring young people. But over time we realized that mentorship isn't only one way—from the adult to the young person. Often the reverse was happening. The young people in our community have to navigate and overcome unthinkable challenges, ranging from gang activity to gun violence to a culture of drugs. The skills necessary to survive in a setting like that eclipse anything that many of our adult mentors have ever had to face. So it made sense to treat these relationship as mutual mentoring.

We changed the name of the adult position from *mentor*, which had been in place for many years, to *listener*. We weren't denying the need to have stable mentors who would become part of the larger adult network surrounding these young people. But by changing the name to *listener*, we acknowledged that the adults needed to learn too. By listening to what these young people were experiencing and by coming to understand how they were navigating challenging circumstances, adults were entering into a relationship that was as transformational for them as it was for the young people.

This principle is true in my life as well. I love Sundays with my community and am very busy from early in the morning until the completion of our service. But what happens next is the highlight of my week. The young people take over the building thirty minutes after the service ends, and they hang out there for the rest of the afternoon. I just sit with them and listen to them talk. Their resilience and creativity consistently amaze me, and I learn much from them every Sunday. I feel like the luckiest guy in the world to have access to so many young people, and I wish that for you as well. If you don't have access to young people—especially young people in the midst of dangerous and challenging social realities—I strongly recommend searching for a church or organization that you can partner with. The lessons you'll learn will be priceless.

Commit to Strong, Persistent, and Determined Action

I so love the encounter between Nicodemus and Jesus, and I've carried the content of that conversation in my heart for a lot of years now: "Very truly I tell you, no one can see the kingdom of God unless they are born again" (John 3:3).

The center of all these conversations on race, justice, reconciliation, and cultural identity remains eternally the same: Jesus Christ. I believe the kingdom of God is the central priority of Jesus. I believe that being born again is a beautiful invitation to a baptism into a new reality with Christ. I also believe that if we're going to take seriously the process of awakening, we must prepare to dig in for the long haul. While I don't want to discourage anyone from boldly moving forward, I'm tempted to say that it's not worth stepping into this journey unless you're ready to follow Jesus all the way to the end.

Dr. Martin Luther King Jr.'s "Letter from Birmingham Jail" deeply touched the nation. Writing on April 16, 1963, King was unusually vulnerable about the hurt he felt toward the indifference and even criticism that he received from the white Christian community. Leaving himself wide open, King shared this:

> I must confess that over the past few years I have been gravely disappointed with the white moderate. I have almost reached the regrettable conclusion that the Negro's great stumbling block in his stride toward freedom is not the White Citizen's Counciler or the Ku Klux Klanner, but the white moderate . . . who constantly says: "I agree with you in the goal you seek, but I cannot agree with your methods of direct action"; who paternalistically believes he can set the timetable for another man's freedom; who lives by a mythical concept of time and who constantly advises the Negro to wait for a "more convenient season . . ." Shallow understanding from people of good will is more frustrating than absolute misunderstanding from people of ill will. Lukewarm acceptance is much more bewildering than outright rejection.

These words are haunting for me, and they serve as a constant reminder of the dangers of a halfhearted pursuit of cultural identity.

While most of us would like to live under the illusion that the great threat to racial progress is the "bad" white people, King dispels that. Even back in 1963, he was clear that it was not the "bad" people of the

White Citizens' Council or the Ku Klux Klan that were the greatest threat to progress but instead the "white moderate," who often demonstrated "shallow understanding" and "lukewarm acceptance." For King, halfhearted commitment was far more confusing than absolute rejection. He then added an important commentary:

> I had hoped that the white moderate would see this need. Perhaps I was too optimistic; perhaps I expected too much. I suppose I should have realized that few members of the oppressor race can understand the deep groans and passionate yearnings of the oppressed race, and still fewer have the vision to see that injustice must be rooted out by strong, persistent and determined action.

To put his words in the positive, can we develop the vision to see that "injustice must be rooted out by strong, persistent and determined action"? I believe King was 100 percent right when he said this, and with these brilliant words he left us with a call to full devotion to the kingdom vision of Jesus. To participate in this work, we have to dig in for the long haul. We have to take seriously that life as we know it is a battle between two competing kingdoms and that we must be strong, we must be persistent, and we must be determined.

Follow in the Footsteps of the Pioneer

Following Jesus into an awakening of cultural identity requires a life of robust faith. That's why an image I often come back to for sustenance in the journey is this: "Therefore, since we are surrounded by such a great cloud of witnesses, let us throw off everything that hinders and the sin that so easily entangles. And let us run with perseverance the race marked out for us, fixing our eyes on Jesus, the pioneer and perfecter of faith" (Hebrews 12:1-2).

There's a lot I love about this passage. I love that there's a great cloud of witnesses that has gone before us, and they now surround us with prayer, cheering us on as we press forward. I love (as well as loathe) the reminder that sin so easily hinders us, requiring us to repent and refresh regularly. I love the reminder that we must run this race with perseverance.

As much as I love each of those truths, what I most love is the description of Jesus as the *pioneer* of our faith. A pioneer leads the way into unchartered territory and thus creates a path for others to follow.

Isn't that an inspiring way to think about the role of faith in our cultural identity journey? It reminds me that sustenance for the journey doesn't come from inside me. The courage, the strength, the wisdom, the humility, the direction—they all come from Jesus. He is the pioneer of this faith journey, and he is the one who charts the course. My job is to listen for his voice and then to follow him bravely as he blazes the trail. I can't see the master plan or precisely where he's leading me, but I can see him carving out the path right in front of me. And if I follow, one step at a time, he will protect and guide me into a deeper awakening.

I pray that I will continue to meet Jesus in powerful ways, and I pray that you will too. I pray that you are able to throw off everything that hinders you from moving forward. I pray that you fix your eyes on Jesus, the pioneer of your faith. And I pray that, in return, he opens your eyes to see his kingdom in ways that go beyond what you could ever imagine.

Discussion Questions

Chapter 1: The Day I Discovered My World Was White

1. Daniel told his friend at the wedding that as a white person, he wished he had a culture too. His friend responded by saying, "White culture is very real. In fact, when white culture comes in contact with other cultures, it almost always wins." How do you feel when you hear that response? What do you suppose this friend was trying to suggest when he said this?

2. Do you agree with the idea that white culture tends to "win" when it comes into contact with other cultures? How do you see this playing out in your own experience?

3. In the chapter, Daniel expresses resistance to the idea that his culture is "white." If you are white, in what ways are you influenced by your specific cultural background (e.g., Irish, Italian, etc.) and in what ways are you influenced by being white in America?

4. Do you have any resistance to the idea that "white" is a primary cultural identity in the United States? Why or why not?

5. Have you ever experienced a moment where you realized how much white culture influences American culture? What was this experience like?

6. What elements do you associate with white culture in America? What elements of white culture are obvious to most people? What elements are not?

7. Daniel's friend said, "Just because certain white individuals demonstrate prejudice or racism by their behaviors doesn't implicate an entire race." What do you think his friend meant?

8. In the aftermath of his wedding experience, Daniel describes the internal conflict between his individual responsibility and his responsibility as a white person in America. Have you ever experienced this conflict? What are your initial ideas about the interplay between individual and corporate responsibility?

9. Daniel's mentor asked him to catalog the voices that had shaped him as a person. Try this activity for yourself. First, list the individuals who have significantly influenced you. Then take note of their cultural backgrounds. Do you notice any patterns? What conclusions might you draw from this exercise?

Chapter 2: Flying Blind

1. In this chapter, Daniel cites statistics on the hypersegregation of the American church from the book *Divided by Faith*. Does this level of segregation surprise you? Why do you think churches tend to be so segregated?

2. Despite his intentions, Daniel's Metro 212 ministry was culturally homogenous. Why do you think his group ended up being all white? Why do you think his initial attempts to increase diversity failed?

3. Have you ever tried to increase the diversity of a group (ethnically or otherwise)? What was the outcome? How did it make you feel? What lessons did you learn?

4. Daniel describes his meeting with a diverse group of Chicago pastors and the hard, but important, words that each shared with him. Do you think these criticisms were fair? How do you think you would have responded?

5. In the story of Nicodemus and Jesus, Nicodemus seems to want a concrete answer from Jesus about what he should do next. Have you ever experienced a situation where you wanted a clear, concrete answer from God but God did not comply? How did it make you feel? How did you react?

6. Do you think white Christians tend to prioritize action over inner transformation? Try to think of a time when you initiated action before contemplation. What did you learn? How might we grow in our ability to see before we act?

7. What might Daniel have needed to see before attempting to lead a multicultural ministry?

8. In what ways might white Americans be blind to racial dynamics? What connections are there between the blindness described in this chapter and the failure to *see* white as a culture (think back to Daniel's conversation at the wedding)?

9. Daniel highlights three terms from the Nicodemus story: *see*, *transform*, and *born again*. Reflecting on your own spiritual journey, think of a time when you struggled with failure or loss. What did God help you *see*? What did God *transform*? In what way(s) were you *born again*?

10. Now think about your own journey with issues of race and culture. What is God helping you to *see*? What is God *transforming*? How might you be *born again*?

Chapter 3: What is Cultural Identity?

1. How would you have defined cultural identity before reading this chapter? Compared with your individual identity, how much have you thought about your cultural identity?

2. Take a few minutes to reflect on Daniel's questions: "Who am I?" and "Where do I fit in the world?" How would you answer those

questions now? How would you have answered them in the past?

3. When you think about your own identity, is your racial or cultural background a key component? Why do you think this is/is not the case?

4. In this chapter, Daniel includes a story about a crosscultural interaction between two eighth grade girls from Beverly Tatum's book *Why Are All of the Black Kids Sitting Together in the Cafeteria?* Have you ever experienced a crosscultural interaction gone wrong? How did it make you feel? What did you learn (either at the time or upon later reflection) from the experience?

5. Daniel gives a number of examples of the normalization of white culture. Did these make sense to you? Can you think of additional instances that you've experienced? How do you think white Americans can learn to see their culture as a part of the larger white culture and not necessarily the standard for *normal*?

6. In the story shared in this chapter, William tried to encourage Jonathan by emphasizing that he didn't see him as culturally different. Daniel suggests that William missed the point of Jonathan's lament. How might discounting the cultural identity of a person of color diminish them? Can you think of other ways that American culture might discount the cultural identity of people of color?

7. Do you agree that one of the privileges of being white in American is the "ability to walk away"? When have you been tempted to walk away from a difficult racial or cultural conversation?

8. What strategies could you use to keep from exercising the privilege of walking away from the conversation? How can spiritual practices play a role in this discipline?

9. As you interact with the biblical examples of the importance of cultural identity in this chapter, what resonates most with you? Why?

10. Do you agree that God calls us to understand our own cultural identity? If so, what choices could you commit to today that might help you continue (or begin) your journey?

Chapter 4: Encounter

1. Describe your first encounter with race. What was your first encounter with the idea of race? Can you link your encounter to the idea of the normalization of whiteness?

2. When you encounter race, what is your first, instinctive reaction? Are you satisfied with the reaction that you tend to have, or do you wish it were different? Why?

3. Before reading this chapter, how familiar were you with the differences between *race* and *ethnicity*? Did you learn anything new about the racial history of America? What, if anything, do you find surprising?

4. This chapter surveys the racialized history of America. Why do you think that Daniel decided to include information about the past? What can we learn about our shared history that might affect how we move forward?

5. This chapter begins with the idea of encountering race at an individual, person-to-person level and then tackles an encounter with race at a broader, systemic level. Do you think it is more difficult to recognize individual-level racism or system-level racism? Why?

6. In what ways do you see racism as a spiritual problem? As a spiritual problem, how might a Christian uniquely fight against racism?

7. In this chapter, Daniel emphasized the importance of the narrative of racial difference. What was your reaction to that concept? What are some of the ways that you can see the narrative of racial difference impacting your everyday life?

8. Daniel suggests that we need to embrace our cultural identity while rejecting the narrative of racial difference. How do you personally reconcile these two ideas?

9. In chapter two, Daniel discussed the hypersegregation of the church. What are some of the ways that the narrative of racial difference may play a role in this segregation?

10. As you think about moving forward in your journey to understand cultural/racial identity, what are your concerns or fears? What motivates you to continue the journey?

Chapter 5: Denial

1. Daniel shared a story of seeing a police officer exhibit racist behavior, but then finding a way to distance himself from the feelings of pain and sorrow it aroused in him. When have you experienced something similar to this?

2. When we witness instances of racial injustice, what factors make it easier or more difficult to speak up?

3. As Daniel points out, many of us have had interactions with people who have racist (or other prejudicial) views. In these cases, what excuses might one use to rationalize these attitudes? Do you think rationalization or denial makes one complicit? Why or why not?

4. Can you think of a time that God has shaken your foundation? What did you learn from that experience?

5. In this chapter, Daniel introduces the phrase "white trauma." What are your reactions to this idea? Do you see evidence of white trauma in institutions or groups that you are a part of? What about within yourself?

6. Daniel gives a number of examples of the American tendency to turn a blind eye toward historical examples of racism. Is reading about

these (sometimes very violent) examples of racism uncomfortable for you? How do you usually respond to examples of extreme injustice?

7. In the Old Testament, God instructs the Israelites to look at a figure of a serpent in order to be healed of their trauma. How might white Americans look at their trauma around race? How could you, personally, take steps to look at your trauma?

8. Confronting trauma is a difficult and potentially exhausting task. What strategies might one use to keep from getting overwhelmed? What role does your spiritual life relationship with God play in this process? What role could it play?

9. What role do you think our communities of faith might play in helping us to personally avoid denial and look at our trauma around race issues? How might we as individuals encourage our communities of faith to do the same?

10. Take a minute to reflect on your own experiences around race. Can you think of times when you have used denial as a strategy to avoid an uncomfortable reality?

Chapter 6: Disorientation

1. Daniel opens this chapter with the story of the blind man who was healed by Jesus. Although Jesus had healed him, the man was not able to see clearly at first. Can you relate to this experience? Outside of your experiences with race, can you think of another time when you were disoriented by being able to see something for the first time?

2. If you have ever experienced disorientation specifically around race, what was that experience like?

3. Like the woman in this chapter's opening story, do you think you have ever gotten too much of your sense of self-worth from being white?

4. Daniel proposes four reasons for disorientation, and the first is a lack of exposure. Take a moment to reflect on your own exposure to other racial and cultural groups. How segregated was your social network growing up?

5. The second proposed reason for disorientation is low stamina. Daniel borrows Robin DiAngelo's concept of race-based stress and suggests that white Americans rarely have to experience this type of stress. What about you? Are you typically drained after a discussion around race? If so, how do you cope with this feeling?

6. In the section on theological understanding, Daniel mentions the often-heard comment that Christ should be at the center instead of race or justice issues. How have you wrestled with reconciling racial or cultural identity issues with identity in Christ?

7. The new member at Daniel's church asked the question, "How did I grow up in a Bible-believing church yet never once learned about the ministry of reconciliation?" What about you? Have you been a part of communities of faith that discuss the idea of reconciliation? If not, why do you think this is the case? If so, describe the experience.

8. The final proposed reason for disorientation is that confrontation of racial issues causes an identity crisis. How do you think whiteness and the narrative of racial difference have played a role in informing your identity? What parts of your identity would be threatened if you stepped further into the journey to understand race?

9. Daniel makes the case that a resilient person can recover, persist, and thrive when disoriented. Do you consider yourself a resilient person? What evidence do you see (or not see) that supports your assessment?

10. If resilience is what allows white Americans to persist in their journeys to understand race, how can we cultivate resilience in ourselves and in our faith communities?

Chapter 7: Shame

1. Have you ever been tempted to stop thinking of yourself as white, like Jeremy in the opening story? What were the reasons?

2. Take some time to reflect on the words *guilt* and *shame*. Have these words ever described your experience with race or culture? What prompted the feeling? How did you deal with it?

3. Brené Brown suggests that guilt might have some positive outcomes and could instigate transformation. Do you agree? When have you had an experience in which guilt yielded a positive outcome?

4. Daniel uses Brown's definition of shame: "believing that we are flawed and therefore unworthy of love and belonging." Think of a time when you have felt this way. How did the feeling of shame affect your relationship with others? How did it affect your relationship with God?

5. Do you ever go into "action-mode" when it might be more appropriate to spend some time lamenting or mourning? If so, why do you think that you react in that way?

6. Before reading this chapter, what was your understanding of lament? In your spiritual life, do you think that you have emphasized praise more than lament? When have you experienced lament?

7. In thinking about your church experiences, do you agree that the white American church has a poor understanding of lament? Where have you seen the link between a lack of lament and an inability to contend with shame in a healthy way?

8. When you consider the idea of lamenting racial injustice without the expectation of reversing it, how do you feel? In what ways might this be challenging to practice?

9. Daniel suggests that white Christians can use the image of a funeral to help guide their practice of lament. Do you find this image helpful? Why or why not?

10. Now that you have read this chapter, how might you, personally, apply the practice of lament when you are feeling shame around your whiteness?

Chapter 8: Self-Righteousness

1. In the introduction to this chapter, Daniel shares a story about a time that self-righteousness diminished his ability to apply the idea of grace to his own life. When have you experienced something like this?

2. Do you feel like you are able to identify self-righteousness in yourself when it begins to inevitably appear? How do you go about doing so? How does your community play a role?

3. Daniel shares a quote from Robin DiAngelo that describes white people's feelings that racism is about being good or bad. Do you find yourself framing it this way? Can you think of an example?

4. This chapter asserts that we protect ourselves from the weight of genuine self-examination by focusing on certain behaviors over others. Has this ever been true of you? How might this practice keep one from reflecting honestly?

5. If it is true that we all need to think of ourselves as moral, how does the threat of holding even subtle or implicit racist ideas challenge this? Why is it difficult to be at peace if your sense of your own morality is challenged?

6. Daniel outlines a number of pitfalls of self-righteousness, including the idea that self-righteousness undermines healthy identity development. Do you resonate with this idea? How can you connect this to your own journey?

7. This chapter contends that when we label people as either "good" (not racist) or "bad" (racist) white people, we undermine attempts at dismantling racism. Do you agree with this? If so, what are some

of the ways that you see this particular form of self-righteousness undermining our efforts?

8. Daniel urges us to view repentance as applicable not only to individual actions but to societal problems as well. What did you think about that claim? How might applying repentance to social ills expand or change our view of repentance?

9. Daniel suggests that it is not enough to focus on isolating individual behavior when confronting racist ideology. Instead of struggling to be identified as a "good white person," he says we should focus on repenting of the ways that the toxic effects of the narrative of racial difference have influenced each one of us. Does this change the way you think about repentance at all, particularly when it comes to our complicity with racial ideologies? Does this provoke ideas for next steps in your own journey? How might you apply this idea to your own identity development?

Chapter 9: Awakening

1. Daniel outlines seven markers that confirm the positive movement in the direction of racial awakening. What was your overall reaction to these seven markers?

2. Of the seven markers explored in this chapter, which one did you most resonate with? Which of the seven markers is most applicable to the next stage of your cultural identity journey?

3. The first marker explored in this chapter is the need to be *theologically* awake. Where do you feel you are when it comes to having a theological conviction around cultural identity and racial justice? This section also noted the importance of holding together activism and evangelism, protest and prayer, personal piety and social justice, intimacy with Jesus and proximity to the poor. How easy or difficult is it for you to hold these together?

4. The second marker is an awakening to the kingdom battle between the doctrine of the imago Dei and the narrative of racial difference, a concept that has been explored at multiple points throughout the book. Do you agree that that this is indeed one of the great battles of our day? How would you describe your own awakening process through the lens of the contest between the imago Dei and the narrative of racial difference?

5. Within this second marker is also an exploration of the dangers of portraying Jesus exclusively as a white male. Do you agree that doing so is dangerous? Why or why not? In what ways might this perpetuate the narrative of racial difference?

6. The third marker is a reduced defensiveness about white supremacy. Daniel says this is one of the most important markers of all. How do you feel about that claim? Within this marker he emphasized that we must learn to make the distinction between *individuals* who are white—and thus are eternally valuable to God—from the *system* of white supremacy, which is evil and must be fought on every front. Do you agree with this distinction? How do you assess your own ability to distinguish between these two?

7. Under the fourth marker, Daniel observes that when white people experience an initial awakening about race, their instinctive reaction is to seek out ways to diversify their friendship circle. However, he warns that this is potentially dangerous if it is not first rooted in a desire to battle against white supremacy. Do you agree with this assertion? Why or why not? He also urges those who are white to count the cost for people of color before pursuing intentional friendship. Have you ever considered the potential cost for your friends of color? How might this impact the way that you pursue friendships in the future?

8. Daniel suggests that the fifth marker of association with racial awakening is the shift from asking, "What am I supposed to do?"

to asking, "How well do I see?" This shift represents one of the main themes of the book. Do you agree that this shift is important? What are the potential ramifications of failing to make this shift? Where do you see this shift happening in your own life?

9. The sixth marker is learning to recognize privilege faster and with greater precision. As an illustration, Daniel describes noticing the difference in the ways that his neighbors respond to him as a white person and the ways that they respond to people of color. What are the concrete ways that you have recognized privilege in your life?

10. The final marker is living in a state of hopeful lament. Within this Daniel suggests, "To be white in this country and to be relatively conscious is to be in a state of lament almost all the time." What do you think he is getting at? Do you agree? Why or why not? Daniel then contrasts optimism and hope. What do you see as the difference between these? What does it look like in everyday life to both lament and hope?

Chapter 10: Active Participation

1. In this chapter Daniel outlines ten concrete action steps we can take in response to our growing sense of racial awakening. What was your overall reaction to these ten suggestions? Which of the action steps is most applicable for you in the next stage of your journey?

2. The first suggestion in this chapter is to look for ways to continue to educate ourselves. Daniel noted that our social location is what tends to most strongly shape our inner convictions and personal biases, and that we must beware of the ways this might inhibit us from interacting with alternative perspectives. Do you agree with this? If so, what perspectives might you need to expose yourself to in the spirit of continuing to educate yourself?

3. The second suggestion is to become proximate to suffering. Would you say this is currently true of you? If not, what are some ways that you could potentially put this suggestion into practice?

4. The third suggestion is to find ways to share your social network. Daniel shared two practical questions within this point: What social capital do I have access to? What are ways that I could spend that social capital for the sake of justice? How would you answer these questions for yourself?

5. The fourth suggestion is to find a place to consistently serve with the implication that this place of service should also carry with it the potential for authentic, crosscultural interaction. Do you currently have a place like this where you serve? If not, are there any opportunities that come to mind?

6. The fifth suggestion is to place yourself under the leadership of people of color. Are there any individuals or environments that would represent the potential for exploring this in your own life? Daniel specifically mentions the importance of having the *will* to stick with it once you commit. How did you feel about this point? What kind of self-reflection do you need to engage in before seeking mentorship from a person of color?

7. The sixth suggestion is to invest in white people. Robin DiAngelo says that one of the casualties of building a sense of white identity on the good/bad binary is that we tend to be quick to distance ourselves from white people who we perceive to fall on the bad/racist side of the binary. How have you seen this tendency play out in your own life? How can investing in these relationships be one of the most concrete ways that we actively participate in the ministry of reconciliation? How does that impact your thought process when you consider the white friends and/or family members in your life who are still early on in the racial awakening process?

8. The seventh suggestion is to learn to locate yourself. Daniel says that while this may sound simple in theory, it tends to be difficult for white people to put in practice. Do you agree with this? Why or why not? How comfortable are you with locating yourself?

9. The eighth suggestion is to become a change agent within your industry. Did you feel that this suggestion was applicable to you? If not, are there ways that you could contextualize this principle for the season of life you are in? If yes, what ideas did it stir within you?

10. The ninth suggestion is to find some young people to build with. In this section Daniel proposes that we shift our understanding of mentoring to include learning from those younger than us, particularly when they have been required to develop survival skills that go beyond what has been necessary for many of us. Did that challenge your view of mentorship at all? What access to these types of relationships do you have? How can you pursue those types of relationships?

11. The tenth suggestion is to commit to strong, persistent, and determined action. In this section Daniel refers to Dr. King's warning that "shallow understanding" and "lukewarm acceptance" from white people is often more frustrating than "absolute misunderstanding from people of ill will." How do you respond to the gravity of that statement? After reading this book, how do you honestly assess your readiness to commit to this type of determined action?

Notes

Chapter 2: Flying Blind

[1] Michael O. Emerson, *People of the Dream: Multiracial Congregations in the United States* (Princeton, NJ: Princeton University Press, 2008), 41.

[2] Ibid.

[3] "Mission and Vision: The Eight Core Principles of the Center for Action and Contemplation," Center for Action and Contemplation, https://cac.org/about-cac/missionvision.

Chapter 3: What Is Cultural Identity?

[1] Beverly Tatum, *Why Are All the Black Kids Sitting Together in the Cafeteria?*, rev. ed. (New York: Basic Books, 2003), 20.

[2] Sherwood G. Lingenfelter and Marvin K. Mayers, *Ministering Cross-Culturally: A Model for Effective Personal Relationships* (Grand Rapids: Baker Books, 2016), Kindle loc. 5.

[3] Richard Brislin and Tomoko Yoshida, *Intercultural Communication Training: An Introduction* (Thousand Oaks, CA: Sage, 1994), 118.

[4] Tatum, *Why Are All the Black Kids*, Kindle loc. 59.

[5] W. E. B. Du Bois, *The Souls of Black Folk* (New York: Dover Publications, 1903), 2.

[6] Alistair Bonnett, "White Studies: The Problems and Projects of a New Research Agenda," *Theory, Culture & Society* 13, no. 2 (1996): 146.

Chapter 4: Encounter

[1] David Roediger, *The Wages of Whiteness: Race and the Making of the American Working Class* (Brooklyn, NY: Verso Books, 2007), 72.

[2]Dictonary.com, s.v. "white supremacy," dictionary.com/browse/white-su premacy.

[3]Italics added. Read the entire Declaration of Independence at www.consti tutionfacts.com/us-declaration-of-independence/read-the-declaration. The sentence referring to natives as "merciless Indian savages" is at the end.

[4]Italics added. National Archives, "America's Founding Documents: Consti-tution," www.archives.gov/exhibits/charters/constitution_transcript.html.

[5]Gregory Rodriguez, "Mongrel America," *The Atlantic*, January/February 2003, www.theatlantic.com/magazine/archive/2003/01/mongrel -america/305956/.

[6]Ibid.

[7]Tal Kopan, "What Donald Trump Has Said About Mexico and Vice Versa," CNN, August 31, 2016, www.cnn.com/2016/08/31/politics/donald-trump -mexico-statements.

[8]Ronald Takaki, *Strangers from a Different Shore: A History of Asian Americans* (New York: Little, Brown, 1998), 101-2.

[9]Beverly Tatum, *Why Are All the Black Kids Sitting Together in the Cafeteria?*, rev. ed. (New York: Basic Books, 2003), 154.

[10]Kenyon Chan and Shirley Hune, "Racialization and Panethnicity: From Asians in America to Asian Americans," in *Toward a Common Destiny: Improving Race and Ethnic Relations in America*, ed. W. D. Hawley and A. W. Jackson (San Francisco: Jossey-Bass, 1995), 210; cited in Tatum, *Why Are All the Black Kids*.

[11]Transcribed from the PBS series *Race—The Power of an Illusion*, episode 3, "The House We Live In," executive producer Larry Adelman (California Newsreel, 2003), www.pbs.org/race/000_About/002_04-about-03.htm.

[12]If you are not yet familiar with his work, learn more about him: he is author of the bestselling *Just Mercy* and founder of the Equal Justice Initiative (eji.org). His speech on injustice, "We Need to Talk About an Injustice," TED, March 2012, can be viewed at www.ted.com/talks/bryan_stevenson_ we_need_to_talk_about_an_injustice?language=en.

[13]Corey G. Johnson, "Bryan Stevenson on Charleston and Our Real Problem with Race," interview with Bryan Stevenson, The Marshall Project, June 24, 2015, www.themarshallproject.org/2015/06/24/bryan-stevenson-on -charleston-and-our-real-problem-with-race.

[14]C. S. Lewis, *The Weight of Glory and Other Essays* (San Francisco: Harper, 1976), 46.

Chapter 5: Denial

[1] If you're interested in immersing yourself in a more accurate view of how America was discovered, consider reading Mark Charles's *Truth Be Told*, coauthored by Soong-Chan Rah, which explores the Doctrine of Discovery.

[2] "Lynching in America: Confronting the Legacy of Racial Terror," Equal Justice Initiative, 2nd ed., 2015, http://eji.org/lynchinginamerica.

[3] Carlos Ruiz, "Embodying a Disruptive Journey," in *Intercultural Ministry: Hope for a Changing World*, ed. Grace Ji-Sun Kim and Jann Aldredge-Clanton (Valley Forge, PA: Judson, 2017) 62-63.

[4] Mark Charles, "Doctrine of Discovery: Part II," Red Letter Christians, April 12, 2016, www.redletterchristians.org/doctrine-discovery-part-ii/.

Chapter 6: Disorientation

[1] Christopher Ingraham, "Three Quarters of Whites Don't Have Any Non-White Friends," *Washington Post*, August 25, 2014, www.washingtonpost.com/news/wonk/wp/2014/08/25/three-quarters-of-whites-dont-have-any-non-white-friends.

[2] Robin DiAngelo, "White Fragility," *International Journal of Critical Pedagogy* 3 (2011): 58.

[3] Ibid.

[4] Ibid., 54.

[5] Lecrae, Twitter feed, July 4, 2016, https://twitter.com/lecrae/status/750012773212401665?lang=en.

[6] Daniel Hill, *10:10: Life to the Fullest* (Grand Rapids: Baker Books, 2014). I recommend reading *Surprised by Hope* by N. T. Wright and *Generous Justice* by Timothy Keller if you're looking for a good place to start on this topic.

[7] Hill, *10:10*, 31.

[8] Quoted in Sam Adler-Bell, "Why White People Freak Out When They're Called Out About Race," interview with Robin DiAngelo, Alternet, March 12, 2015, www.alternet.org/culture/why-white-people-freak-out-when-theyre-called-out-about-race.

[9] Amy S. Choi, "PopTech's Andrew Zolli on Resilience and Solving World Problems," *Entrepreneur*, January 9, 2013, www.entrepreneur.com/article/225428.

Chapter 7: Shame

[1] Brené Brown, *Daring Greatly: How the Courage to Be Vulnerable Transforms the Way We Live, Love, Parent, and Lead* (New York: Penguin, 2012), 68-69.

[2]Ibid., 72-73.

[3]Ibid.

[4]Ibid.

[5]Ibid.

[6]Soong-Chan Rah, *Prophetic Lament: A Call for Justice in Troubled Times* (Downers Grove, IL: InterVarsity Press, 2015), 64-65.

[7]Ibid., 68.

[8]Ibid., 57-58.

[9]Brené Brown, "Listening to Shame," TED Talks, March 16, 2012, www .youtube.com/watch?v=psN1DORYYV0.

[10]Rah, *Prophetic Lament*, 45-46; quoting Adele Berlin, *Lamentations* (Louisville: Westminster John Knox, 2004), 24.

[11]Ibid., 47.

[12]Dan Allender, "The Hidden Hope in Lament," *Mars Hill Review* 1 (1994): 25-38.

Chapter 8: Self-Righteousness

[1]As recounted in Susan Krauss Whitbourne, "In-Groups, Out-Groups, and the Psychology of Crowds," *Psychology Today*, December 10, 2010, www .psychologytoday.com/blog/fulfillment-any-age/201012/in-groups-out -groups-and-the-psychology-crowds.

[2]Sam Adler-Bell, "Why White People Freak Out When They're Called Out About Race," interview with Robin DiAngelo, Alternet, March 12, 2015, www.alternet.org/culture/why-white-people-freak-out-when-theyre -called-out-about-race.

Chapter 9: Awakening

[1]A. W. Tozer, *The Knowledge of the Holy* (New York: HarperCollins, 1978), 1.

[2]I acknowledge that some argue that the primary point of this passage is how Christians treat one another. But I still propose that, even if that is the interpretation one takes, it's still connected to a theological awakening in regard to cultural identity, reconciliation, and ministering to those on the margins.

[3]Reggie Williams, from a lecture with a group of Christian community development leaders, River City Community Church, Chicago, June 9, 2016.

[4]Nikki Toyama-Szeto explored this concept within her plenary talk on September 1, 2016, at the CCDA National Conference.

[5]Timothy Keller, "Do You See Anything?" (sermon, Redeemer Presbyterian Church, New York, NY, June 18, 2006).

[6]"Interview: Cornel West," *Frontline*, 1997, www.pbs.org/wgbh/pages /frontline/shows/race/interviews/west.html.

Chapter 10: Active Participation

[1]Request membership in Be the Bridge to Racial Unity at www.facebook .com/groups/BetheBridge.

[2]"Wright Edelman Speaks on Children and Poverty," Belmont University, February 5, 2009, http://news.belmont.edu/wright-edelman-speaks-on -children-and-poverty.

[3]Martin Saunders, "Bryan Stevenson: Four Steps to Really Change the World," *Christian Today*, July 16, 2015, www.christiantoday.com/article /bryan.stevenson.four.steps.to.really.change.the.world/59211.htm.

[4]Lauren Rubenstein, "Honorary Degree Recipient Bryan Stevenson Delivers 2016 Commencement Speech," Wesleyan University, May 22, 2106, www .newsletter.blogs.wesleyan.edu/2016/05/22/bryanstevenson2016.

[5]Shane Claiborne, *The Irresistible Revolution: Living as an Ordinary Radical* (Grand Rapids: Zondervan, 2006), 48.

[6]To learn more about Lighthouse Covenant Church, go to lighthousempls .org.

[7]Dee McIntosh, "How Then Shall We Respond" (sermon, Genesis Covenant Church, Maple Grove, MN, December 13, 2015), http://genesiscov.org /sundays/sermons/media-item/103/how-then-shall-we-respond.

[8]Ibid.

[9]See River City Community Development Center, www.rcitycdc.org.

[10]Paul Gorski, "The Myth of the Culture of Poverty," *Educational Leadership* 65, no. 7 (2008); www.ascd.org/publications/educational-leadership/apr08 /vol65/num07/The-Myth-of-the-Culture-of-Poverty.aspx.

[11]Sam Adler-Bell, "Why White People Freak Out When They're Called Out About Race," interview with Robin DiAngelo, Alternet, March 12, 2015, www.alternet.org/culture/why-white-people-freak-out-when-theyre -called-out-about-race.

[12]Ibid.

[13]"Christena Cleveland on Leadership and Sociological Imagination," Fuller Theological Seminary, published July 7, 2015, www.youtube.com /watch?v=q1XMcAAXXXg.

[14]"Christena Cleveland on Embodying Mutuality," Fuller Theological Seminary, published July 7, 2015, www.youtube.com/watch?v=bpoSuhTgjIg.
[15]Ibid.

C|C   CHRISTIAN COMMUNITY
D|A   DEVELOPMENT ASSOCIATION

The Christian Community Development Association (CCDA) is a network of Christians committed to engaging with people and communities in the process of transformation. For over twenty-five years, CCDA has aimed to inspire, train, and connect Christians who seek to bear witness to the Kingdom of God by reclaiming and restoring under-resourced communities. CCDA walks alongside local practitioners and partners as they live out Christian Community Development (CCD) by loving their neighbors.

CCDA was founded in 1989 under the leadership of Dr. John Perkins and several other key leaders who are engaged in the work of Christian Community Development still today. Since then, practitioners and partners engaged in the work of the Kingdom have taken ownership of the movement. Our diverse membership and the breadth of the CCDA family are integral to realizing the vision of restored communities.

The CCDA National Conference was birthed as an annual opportunity for practitioners and partners engaged in CCD to gather, sharing best practices and seeking encouragement, inspiration, and connection to other like-minded Christ-followers who are committed to ministry in difficult places. For four days, the CCDA family, coming from across the country and around the world, is reunited around a common vision and heart.

Additionally, the CCDA Institute serves as the educational and training arm of the association, offering workshops and trainings in the philosophy of CCD. We have created a space for diverse groups of leaders to be steeped in the heart of CCD and forge lifelong friendships over the course of two years through CCDA's Leadership Cohort.

CCDA has a long-standing commitment to the confrontation of injustice. Our advocacy and organizing is rooted in Jesus' compassion and commitment to Kingdom justice. While we recognize there are many injustices to be fought, as an association we are strategically working on issues of immigration, mass incarceration, and education reform.

To learn more, visit www.ccda.org/ivp

More Titles from IVP and CCDA

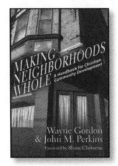

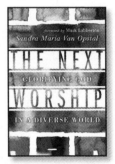

Embrace
978-0-8308-4471-5

**Making
Neighborhoods Whole**
978-0-8308-3756-4

The Next Worship
978-0-8308-4129-5

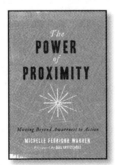

**The Power
of Proximity**
978-0-8308-4390-9

**Where the Cross
Meets the Street**
978-0-8308-3691-8

Please visit us at ivpress.com.

Missio Alliance

Missio Alliance has arisen in response to the shared voice of pastors and ministry leaders from across the landscape of North American Christianity for a new "space" of togetherness and reflection amid the issues and challenges facing the church in our day. We are united by a desire for a fresh expression of evangelical faith, one significantly informed by the global evangelical family. Lausanne's Cape Town Commitment, "A Confession of Faith and a Call to Action," provides an excellent guidepost for our ethos and aims.

Through partnerships with schools, denominational bodies, ministry organizations, and networks of churches and leaders, Missio Alliance addresses the most vital theological and cultural issues facing the North American Church in God's mission today. We do this primarily by convening gatherings, curating resources, and catalyzing innovation in leadership formation.

Rooted in the core convictions of evangelical orthodoxy, the ministry of Missio Alliance is animated by a strong and distinctive theological identity that emphasizes

Comprehensive Mutuality: Advancing the partnered voice and leadership of women and men among the beautiful diversity of the body of Christ across the lines of race, culture, and theological heritage.

Hopeful Witness: Advancing a way of being the people of God in the world that reflects an unwavering and joyful hope in the lordship of Christ in the church and over all things.

Church in Mission: Advancing a vision of the local church in which our identity and the power of our testimony is found and expressed through our active participation in God's mission in the world.

In partnership with InterVarsity Press, we are pleased to offer a line of resources authored by a diverse range of theological practitioners. The resources in this series are selected based on the important way in which they address and embody these values, and thus, the unique contribution they offer in equipping Christian leaders for fuller and more faithful participation in God's mission.

missioalliance.org | twitter.com/missioalliance | facebook.com/missioalliance

More Titles from IVP
and Missio Alliance

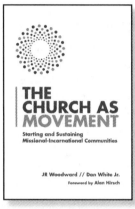

The Church as Movement
978-0-8308-4133-2

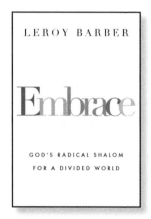

Embrace
978-0-8308-4471-5

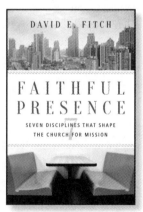

Faithful Presence
978-0-8308-4127-1

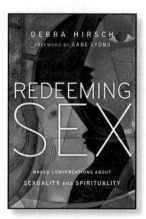

Redeeming Sex
978-0-8308-3639-0

Please visit us at ivpress.com.